HARD QUESTIONS
ON GLOBAL
EDUCATIONAL CHANGE

Hard Questions on Global Educational Change

Policies, Practices, and the Future of Education

Pasi Sahlberg
Jonathan Hasak
Vanessa Rodriguez
and Associates

TEACHERS COLLEGE PRESS
TEACHERS COLLEGE | COLUMBIA UNIVERSITY
NEW YORK AND LONDON

Published by Teachers College Press, 1234 Amsterdam Avenue, New York, NY 10027

Copyright © 2017 by Teachers College, Columbia University

Cover photo by Image Source / Getty Images.

Library of Congress Cataloging-in-Publication Data is available at loc.gov

ISBN 978-0-8077-5818-2 (paper)
ISBN 978-0-8077-5819-9 (hardcover)
ISBN 978-0-8077-7559-2 (ebook)

Printed on acid-free paper
Manufactured in the United States of America

24 23 22 21 20 19 18 178 7 6 5 4 3 2 1

Contents

Acknowledgments

In the summer of 2015, between the 2 academic years at Harvard Graduate School of Education (HGSE), I was looking for ideas for a new course for our master's and doctoral students. In most schools of education around the world, there are not too many options available to study international education issues such as school reforms, teacher policies, or teaching practices in different countries. The other theme often absent in university course catalogues is an inquiry into global educational reform that would provide balanced perspectives to debated questions about policies, practices, and the future of education. I decided, therefore, to offer our students a course titled Hard Questions on Global Educational Change.

There was, however, one condition I set for myself before teaching this course: I didn't want to teach this course alone; I wanted to have one or two others work with me. I was lucky to find two students who were brave enough to take the challenge. Vanessa Rodriguez was, at that time, a doctoral candidate at HGSE, and I was part of her dissertation committee. Jonathan Hasak graduated from HGSE 2 years ago; he was my former student and a current teaching fellow in my other courses.

Before more formal acknowledgements, it is necessary to say a word or two about the course itself. We selected 21 students for this course based on their motivation for and experience with global issues in education. We decided to meet with them weekly for 90 minutes during the entire year in order to create a safer and more comfortable environment in which to learn about complex questions in education. We expected students to learn, among other things, about the most common problems and controversies related to educational reforms, to understand these educational-change questions from international perspectives, to learn to distinguish facts and fiction about difficult educational-change questions, and to leverage social media and other tools for promoting change and sharing ideas.

Near the end of the fall semester, after listening to the students debate and read their essays, we thought these conversations and ideas should be shared more widely than just with the teaching team. There-fore, we gave students two questions to work on during winter break: Would you be ready to write a chapter about one hard question that is close to your heart? What would that question be? That is how the idea of this book was born. All students were excited to be part of this jour-ney that was actually inspired by a book written and edited by Arizona State University professors David Berliner and Gene Glass: *50 Myths and Lies About American Public Schools: The Real Crisis in Education* (Teachers College Press, 2014). In our book we decided to include seven globally discussed controversial questions about educational change.

We worked intensively over the entire spring semester on these seven questions. By making literature reviews, reading current academic and popular texts, interviewing experts and scholars, and writing numerous draft versions, students became truly engaged in learning more and writ-ing better. Limiting the word count available to each student team chal-lenged the authors to focus on clarity and find their own way of writing. How well students succeeded is up to you to judge when you read the rest of the book.

There are many people who deserve to be acknowledged due to their contribution in ensuring that this book saw the light of day. First, I want to thank my coauthors Vanessa Rodriguez and Jonathan Hasak for their companionship during planning and teaching the course upon which this book is based. Without their support and help to the students, this book would not have been possible.

Second, each student separately and the entire class collectively de-serve thanks and praises: Aditi Adhikari, Love Basillote, Jason Brown, Janine Campbell, Chu Chen, Momar Dieng, Fairuz Alia Jamaluddin, Zachary Goldman, Aline Hankey, Amanda Klonsky, Elaine Koh, Lauren Marston, Lauren Owen, Elyse Postlewaite, Wen Qiu, Jonathan Seiden, Reema Souraya, Randy Tarnowski, Terence Tan Wei Ting, Kolja Wohl-leben, and Sharon Yoo. This international class of 15 nationalities, rang-ing from Singapore to Chile and China to the United States, provided rich global perspectives with which to delve into some of the most im-portant questions in education from multiple angles.

Several renowned scholars and thinkers generously made their views and their time available by visiting our classes. Special thanks go to Angelo Gavrielatos, Andy Hargreaves, Stephen Heyneman, Rebecca Holcombe, Phil McRae, Nicholas Negroponte, Diane Ravitch, Sir Ken Robinson, Yong Zhao, Howard Gardner, and Marty West. As part of collecting data for their essays, students also interviewed education spe-cialists around the world. While they are too many to be mentioned here, we sincerely thank them all for helping students to gain deeper understanding of their hard questions.

I also want to thank colleagues at HGSE who made it possible to teach the course that led to this book. Special thanks to my faculty assistant Wendy Angus at HGSE who provided instrumental help and support to us all during the academic year.

No book can ever be completed without the hard work, encouragement, and gentle push of the publisher. I am grateful to Sarah Biondello at Teachers College Press for her excellent eye as editor and for her patience at times when we were making last-minute changes and requests. I have learned, again, new things about writing and also about editing texts of my coauthors from Sarah. Well done indeed!

Finally, and perhaps most importantly, I want to thank my wife, Petra, and our sons, Otto and Noah, who have shared my time with this book longer than I promised it would take. Looking at your own children who are still too young to be at school gives you a particular point of view to educational questions. Each of the hard questions in this book is important for my sons' future as well as for those of millions of other parents. That has been my excuse when I was supposed to be with my family but instead worked on these texts. I know they will understand and accept that, one day.

At the end of the 1-year journey, Vanessa, Jonathan, and I asked our students to put in writing what they had learned with us. This is what one student wrote:

> I've learned that we may never be able to answer some of these questions as a result, but that what's important is that we take the time to gather the information, speak to those involved and consider all sides of the coin, if you will. In fact, I learned that a certain level of discomfort is critical to anyone considering working in international education, and that someone who is closed minded and has made all of their decisions prior to tackling any of the issues would do the field a disservice.

This said, I know I can speak on behalf of all of us involved with this book when I dedicate it to all those young people who choose education, especially teaching other people, as their life career.

—Pasi Sahlberg

CHAPTER 1

How Do Educators Respond to Hard Questions on Educational Change?

We followed the graduation ceremonies of the Harvard Graduate School of Education class of 2016 with mixed feelings. On the one hand, we were proud of these students and their accomplishments during the year. Many of them left behind promising early careers in fields that would have most likely brought them wealth and prosperity to attend the school of education. They had decided to dedicate at least part of their working life to improving education for children and youth in different parts of the world. On the other hand, we were perplexed because we were not sure whether these new graduates actually knew and would be able to follow through on what is necessary in the complex, rapidly changing field of education today. We were saddened to know that only a handful of these hundreds of graduates would go back to the classroom and use their new knowledge to teach children. As they walked in their regalia through the aisles of Longfellow Hall to the Radcliffe Yard to receive their diplomas, did they understand what they didn't yet know? Had we accomplished our goal of teaching them how to deal with hard questions on education?

Our overall aim in teaching students at the graduate school of education is to help them to become changemakers. In the beginning of each course, when asked of postgraduation plans, students commonly answer that they want to change the way education systems and schools operate today. Some envision working through international development organizations, while others intend to become social entrepreneurs and focus on some specific aspect of education, such as children living in poverty or girls' education. Changemakers, we thought, would need some foundational skills to succeed, including understanding the hard questions, the importance of the global education reform movement, and effective op-ed writing. Graduate school programs rarely provide courses on these skills critical for a changemaker.

The world of educational changemakers and others who try to improve current education systems is more complex than ever. Information, knowledge, and skills that young people are expected to possess, understand, and embody are not only continuously increasing but also changing in terms of their significance and relevance for the future. The need to adjust entire education systems quickly to deal with new realities has become obvious around the world; this is also relevant for those education systems that are performing better than most others, but probably the most important single reason for increased complexity in educators' worlds has been the widening canyon between what schools do and how the world works. We now debate whether young people need to host knowledge in similar ways than they did before because Google, Watson, and other technologies can bring all necessary knowledge to us in a blink of an eye (Wagner, 2012). Some argue that because the need for routine skills in labor markets has rapidly declined, many traditional vocational training programs have become irrelevant or redundant. In other words, those working in education—whether in practice, policy, or reform—must have much wider and deeper understandings of social, economic, and political contexts of education. Many essential questions in education today are global in nature (Hargreaves & Shirley, 2012), bringing yet another dimension to the competencies that we expect from education changemakers.

Globalization has also led to synchronization of education systems from an international perspective. This means that similar, if not the same, educational issues are debated and argued from one country to another. Increased global mobility of labor, students, and businesses has brought standardization of curricula, examinations, and qualifications as a central theme in many education policies around the world. The growing cost of education due to increasing enrollment has made efficiency, performance, and accountability the key characteristics that education system leaders in different countries are giving their attention to today. As a consequence, various data-driven education policies are often offered as the way forward. For example, international student assessments, such as Organisation for Economic Co-operation and Development's (OECD) Programme for International Student Assessment (PISA), and surveys about teaching and learning, such as OECD's Teaching and Learning International Survey, or TALIS, are increasingly used as the principal source for national education policies and reforms. Global education statistics and performance indicators are also examples of a data-driven approach that are now common tools of any education expert or changemaker. In this book we call the controversial, complex questions that globally shape education policies and practices *hard questions on educational change*. While these questions are infinite, seven of the most pressing are included in this book. We encourage readers to phrase new hard questions and use them in expanding your own understanding of education.

THREE FOUNDATIONAL SKILLS THAT EDUCATION CHANGEMAKERS NEED

There are no international standards or common expectations for what graduates from schools of education should know and be able to do. One reason is that graduate programs in education are very different in their scope and content depending on education systems and universities. Some students, like the chapter authors of this book, earned their master's degrees after studying 1 year at a graduate school of education. Many of their peers in other universities in the United States have spent 2 years and, therefore, studied a wider range of courses in education. Education school graduates in Finland, for example, have typically studied 5 years and written two research-based theses for their degree (Sahlberg, 2015). In the United States and most other countries, new graduates in education complete their degrees with significantly different knowledge and skill sets. We argue that regardless of the program, degree, or university, present-day education changemakers need to possess three essential skill sets that are not systematically required today: identify and cope with hard questions on educational change, understand global trends and their drivers, and write clear and convincing opinion-based essays.

The Importance of Understanding Hard Questions

Education has become increasingly politicized with the growing involvement by commercial interest groups. This is true not just in the United States but around the world. In particular, educational research and educational change knowledge, that is what makes educational reforms work, have increasingly been influenced by funders that now include corporations, philanthropists, think tanks, and various national and international organizations. As a consequence—particularly when issues of school choice, standardized testing, the teaching profession, data-driven governance and accountability, educational technology, or perceiving education as commodity and private good arise—the evidence becomes situational and fragile (Mundy, Green,

Lingard, & Verger, 2016). The purpose of this book is to bring more light to some of the hard questions in today's education debates and, therefore, raise awareness of the subjective nature of evidence in policy making.

In the past 30 years, countries around the world have diverged in their approaches towards governance, curriculum, funding, and leadership, positioning themselves along a spectrum from public, state-based to market-based economic approaches. Broadly, state-based approaches can include models that view education primarily as public good over market competition. Governments in these countries—Nordic countries, Canada, or Germany—typically levy higher tax rates used to provide better and more equal social services such as health care and education. On the other side of the political and economic spectrum, market-based policies encourage competition between private firms and public organizations to provide educational services. This is known as the neoliberal approach, and it is favored in England, some parts of Australia, increasingly the United States, and now in the developing world in Liberia, Kenya, and Philippines, for example. This approach privileges deregulation and use of public funding to support private entities and public-private partnerships for their delivery of education and other public goods (Adamson, Åstrand, & Darling-Hammond, 2016). Internationally comparable education data that is now available can facilitate an analysis of the strengths and weaknesses of these different approaches.

In the past 15 years, data from new international student assessments, especially that of PISA administered by the OECD, has created a whole new geography of educational performance. Many of the previous international education models have lost their place to new countries and systems that have demonstrated high performance in these benchmark surveys. Data from PISA and other comparable international statistics together with case studies and surveys that include entire education system (jurisdictions or countries) now provide an alternative way to discuss and debate some of the central policy questions in education.

In an era where private enterprises leverage new complex evaluation systems to market their educational reform interests, changemakers need to be savvy consumers of data and policy. Most importantly, education experts and those aiming at improving education should have sufficient knowledge to identify and skills to cope with hard questions on educational change. This means that changemakers should

- utilize research to identify successful models of educational change;
- be able to formulate new critical questions based on that change knowledge and research;

- understand the major arguments from both sides of these critical questions; and
- write convincingly to both professionals and the general public about hard questions on educational reform.

The Importance of Knowing the Global Education Reform Movement

You may be able to teach in the classroom or lead a school without too much understanding of what the world of education outside your own school looks like. However, we argue that we live in such an interconnected world at the moment that even grassroots-level practitioners benefit from having at least a basic idea of the worldview of education. Educational theories, teaching methods, curricula, and learning tools are very similar from one education system to another. A closer look at the system-level principles and policies of education reveal even more commonalities between education systems today. We argue that the success of educational reforms increases when the changemakers understand what the primary global trends in educational change are. One critical concept to teach is the *Global Education Reform Movement* (Sahlberg, 2016).

The idea of the Global Education Reform Movement, or GERM as it is also known, first appeared in Andy Hargreaves' research on the standardization movement, which became popular around the world in the 1990s (Hargreaves, Earl, Moore, & Manning, 2001). Hargreaves called this the Global Education Reform Agenda. The term *GERM* was coined in early 2000s after the OECD's PISA became a dominant theme in international education policy conversations. Primarily promoted by the interests of international development agencies and private enterprises, globalization of education policies and reforms were initially inspired by three distinct and well-meaning global educational ideas that aimed to improve quality and equity of education systems around the world (Sahlberg, 2015).

The first is the breakthrough of constructivist approaches to education that gradually shifted the focus from the teacher (instruction or input) to the student (learning or output) beginning in the late 1980s. As a consequence, education reformers and policymakers began to ask for clearer and higher expectations for student learning, curriculum standards, and productive classroom teaching methods. The second is the growing public demand for guaranteed, inclusive education for all pupils that became a prominent global theme in the 1990s. Centrally mandated curricula and learning standards in tandem with aligned national standardized testing and examinations became the main attempts to guarantee that the quality of educational performance for all really took place around the world. The third is decentralization of education governance that brought more autonomy to schools and also increased teachers' freedom to design their teaching in classroom as they saw best. Since the year 2000, decision making began to shift from central offices to local governments and schools (Sahlberg, 2015). Moving power from the center to local communities and schools increased school autonomy and brought along tighter accountability for schools and teachers.

Changemakers should be aware of how GERM manifests itself from one education system to another. The following manifestations have often been the root of hard questions on educational change.

First, and perhaps the most common manifestation of GERM, is increased school choice for parents and the competition between schools for student enrollment that comes with it. Almost all education systems have introduced alternative forms of schooling, offering parents more choice regarding their children's schooling (OECD, 2013). The voucher system in Chile in the 1980s, free schools in Sweden in the 1990s, charter schools in the United States in the 2000s, and secondary academies in England in the 2010s are examples of faith in competition as an engine of advancement. At the same time, evidence has shown that the proportion of more advantaged students studying in private schools or independent schools has grown. In Australia, for example, nearly every third primary and secondary school student studies in nongovernmental schools (Jensen, 2013). School league tables that rank schools based on their performance in national standardized assessments have further increased competition between schools. OECD data show that, according to school principals across OECD countries, more than three-quarters of the students assessed by PISA attend schools that compete with at least one other school for enrollment. Finally, students, especially in many Asian countries, experience stronger pressure to perform better against their peers due to a tough race for the best high schools and universities.

The second manifestation is *standardized testing* as the main means for accountability; in other words, holding teachers and schools accountable for students' achievement through external standardized test scores. School performance—especially raising students' measured achievement—is intimately tied to the processes of evaluating, inspecting, and rewarding or punishing schools and teachers. Performance-based pay, data walls in teachers' lounges, and school rankings in newspapers are examples of new accountability mechanisms that often draw their data primarily from external standardized student tests and teacher evaluations. The United States' growing infatuation with the performance-based pay scale and accountability based on standardized test results relies upon two heatedly debated assumptions. First, teachers will work harder for extra pay. Second, test scores are the largest factor in determining effective teachers. Using this logic, if a teacher is boasting stellar student test scores, she must be working diligently, teaching successfully, and worthy of higher pay. It is this thinking that contributes to the undermining of the teaching profession in certain countries across the globe. The problem with this overreliance on standardized tests is not that students, teachers, and schools are held accountable using data from knowledge tests, per se, but rather the way inappropriate accountability mechanisms affect teachers' work and students' learning. Whenever school accountability relies on poor-quality and low-cost standardized tests, as is currently the case in many places, accountability becomes what is left when responsibility is subtracted.

The third manifestation of GERM comes through educational reforms that lead to the privatization of public schools (Adamson, Åstrand, & Darling-Hammond, 2016). The rush to enhance parental choice and improve efficiency and productivity in the quest for education excellence has brought various providers of education alongside public schools around the world. This well-known theory of change, based on economic models of Milton Friedman, maintains that parents must be given the freedom to choose their children's education and thereby encourage healthy competition among schools so they better serve families' diverse needs. Typically, school choice manifests itself through the emergence of private schools where parents pay tuition for their children's education. Today, privatization of public schools and universities is more popular than ever before, as scores of various fee-based and publicly funded private schools and universities expand choice in education markets. Charter schools in the United States, free schools in Sweden, upper secondary school academies in England, religious schools in the Netherlands, and various for-profit private operators in developing countries are examples of mechanisms to advance parental choice. Privately funded schooling ideology maintains that education should be a commodity just like the hospitality industry or housing markets where parents can use the public funds set aside for their children's education—public or private—in a way that works best for them.

Other manifestations of GERM include a stronger focus on basic knowledge and skills, namely reading, literacy, mathematics, and science; de-professionalizing teaching and learning that often includes abolishing teacher unions and associations; and using technology to replace teachers and schools as media of teaching and learning. Education policies and reforms that aim at sustainable educational change must be built on good awareness and understanding of these global change forces that often counter what changemakers aim to accomplish.

The Importance of Writing About Your Opinion

Schools of education often aim to prepare their graduates to change the world. The challenge, however, is that typical means of communicating educational reform knowledge are too slow and too weak to make an impact. Newly trained educators may have knowledge about what to do, but they often don't know how to influence others.

Outside of academia, effective contemporary education writing no longer needs to take a long and winding road toward traditional publication. Instead, op-eds (opposite the editorial page in newspapers), blogs, and social media outlets have become expedient ways to reach an audience with a short attention span that increasingly consumes its information on mobile devices. In order to elevate educator voices in global education debates, educators should be able to embrace this new style of communication—one that is coherent, succinct, and, most importantly, attuned to audience's flagging attention spans.

Our experience in teaching students at graduate schools has suggested that most have an easy time writing extended academic papers but struggle with shorter pieces that express their opinions on educational issues. As a result, these future educators miss an opportunity to influence public opinion and shape practice at a significantly larger scale.

Expressing an opinion has traditionally had no real place in academia, except in informal conversations and debates. Each course we taught at Harvard included an assignment that asked students to take an opinion on an education topic about which they are passionate. We encouraged students to identify hard questions that would easily spark different views but would not have straightforward answers. The only requirement was that the essay should be about 600 words long, no more. Often in reading first drafts of students' op-eds, regardless of how academically strong these students were, we saw that they were much less comfortable presenting their own perspectives and more comfortable citing research and adopting fashionable educational jargon.

In fact, the entire world of opinion-based texts seemed foreign to students. We learned two important lessons that are also important to this book. First, students used more than half of their available writing space providing context, citing others' works, or trying to cover the wider education reform debate. Second, they spent most of their attention emphasizing a diagnosis, such as we need to professionalize the teaching profession, but wrote little about solutions or how exactly they proposed to professionalize the profession.

Perplexed, we started asking ourselves why writing op-eds was so challenging to our students. Perhaps it was carelessness on our part in not providing op-ed writing rubrics, or maybe the fault lay with higher education institutions that ask students without exception to write longer academic papers regardless of whether they are on the research track in their program.

Don't get us wrong. Academic writing is an important skill that all graduate students should master, yet if students are serious about influencing public opinion and advocating for education reforms as changemakers, we believe they should hone their opinion-writing skills as well. The ability to express an opinion clearly and effectively draws on critical thinking, speaking, writing, and reading skills, and graduate students should have these skills by the time they complete their program.

Most students in graduate schools need help embracing their own voice. This is what we did. We ran a class-long workshop for understanding what makes a powerful op-ed. We reminded students that many readers today have short attention spans, and the first paragraph has to be interesting enough to keep them reading further.

We then provided five habits of mind of an op-ed or column writer:

- Think carefully about the point you really want to make, before you start writing, so that you will arrive at a single issue that you succinctly and clearly communicate.
- Embrace your own voice, authority, and experiences. You should be passionate, authentic, and make the reader care about your topic.
- Avoid jargon and generalities, and acknowledge different perspectives.
- Support your opinions with facts. Check them to be sure they are true.
- If you are citing a problem in your essay, you should also offer solutions.

Then comes the key principle of all: We allowed students to rewrite their op-eds, and we provided feedback and comments for as long as students felt the need for further feedback and rewrites. Op-ed assignments typically counted as 15 to 20% of the entire grade. A published op-ed or column in a newspaper or media outlet's online service automatically awarded the student an A.

This has probably been the single most beneficial learning experience for students. We wanted to teach them that writing an op-ed always requires dealing with feedback, critical comments, rewriting, and several rounds of editing. Changemakers, regardless of their level or experience, have to be able to take an editor's and the public's feedback and tolerate critical comments.

Two lessons from teaching students to write opinion-based essays are essential for reading this book. First, writing op-eds to general audiences about educational issues is difficult. It requires different habits of minds and communication skills than typical academic writing. Second, many graduate students believe that although they have views about education, they don't have a voice to have opinions in public debates. We believe that all it takes is one published op-ed in a national newspaper or on a popular blog to change this mind-set dramatically. Finally, teaching new educators and changemakers who aspire to make a difference in the world, we have realized that in a rapidly changing information landscape, they'll make a greater impact if they update their communication skills. Learning how to write a compelling opinion piece is a good place to start.

THIS BOOK

The following chapters describe seven hard questions on global educational change that we think influence the directions of educational reforms around the world. Each chapter is written by a group of three graduate students of the Harvard Graduate School of Education class of 2016. Students had the freedom to choose the style of writing and how to phrase their question. Students did a comprehensive literature review of their topic, interviewed experts, and discussed their manuscript several times with other students. These chapters are not opinions of the authors; rather they are academic essays. The last chapter extends the trajectory of the book by providing considerations to help readers tackle hard questions by exploring emerging hard questions facing modern educational systems.

REFERENCES

Adamson, F., Åstrand, B., & Darling-Hammond, L. (Eds.). (2016). *Global education reform. How privatization and public investment influence education outcomes.* New York, NY: Routledge.

Hargreaves, A., Earl, L., Moore, S., & Manning, S. (2001). *Learning to change. Teaching beyond subjects and standards.* San Francisco, CA: Jossey-Bass.

Hargreaves, A., & Shirley, D. (2012). *The Global Fourth Way. The quest for educational excellence.* Thousand Oaks, CA: Corwin.

Jensen, B. (2013). *The myth of markets in school education*. Melbourne, Australia: Grattan Institute.

Mundy, K., Green, A., Lingard, R., & Verger, A. (Eds.). (2016). *The handbook of global policy and policymaking in education*. New York, NY: Wiley-Blackwell.

OECD. (2013). *PISA 2012 results: What makes schools successful? Resources, policies and practices* (Vol. 4). Paris: OECD.

Sahlberg, P. (2015). *Finnish lessons 2.0: What can the world learn from educational change in finland*. New York, NY: Teachers College Press.

Sahlberg, P. (2016). The Finnish paradox: Equitable public education within a competitive market economy. In F. Adamson, B. Åstrand, & L. Darling-Hammond (Eds.), *Global education reform. How privatization and public investment influence education outcomes* (pp. 130–150). New York, NY: Routledge.

Wagner, T. (2012). *Creating innovators. The making of young people who will change the world*. New York, NY: Scribner's.

CHAPTER 2

Can Parental Choice Improve Education for All?

Janine Campbell, Aline Hankey, and Jonathan Seiden

Few questions in education are as discussed, debated, and researched as that of choice. When faced with the question, "Does parental choice improve educational systems?", we were rather intimidated. Even finding a starting point for our research was a complicated ordeal. In addition to mountains of seemingly contradictory evidence (Have a point of view? There's a study to support that!), we were faced with more fundamental questions: "What exactly is parental choice in education?", "What does it mean for an educational system to improve?", and "How do parents choose?"

We, therefore, begin with a brief overview of the multidimensional nature of parental choice in education. We classify choice as existing on two broad dimensions. *Inherent choice* is a product of society and individual means, while *public policy choice* is intentionally implemented by governments. We explain the historical contexts of both and the economic rationale that has driven many countries to expand public policy choice.

Historically, policies of choice have been evaluated by their effects on student outcomes, educational efficiency, and occasionally equity and parental satisfaction. Evidence exists that choice policies affect each of these measures, but that choice neither destroys nor dramatically improves educational systems. However, while public policy choice is extensively debated and researched, discussions rarely consider the individual and *how* and *why* parents make educational decisions. We believe that a deeper understanding of how people choose, in addition to traditional economic theories, is essential for policymakers. We will, therefore, consider theories from behavioral economics, identity economics, and mental models to conceptualize choice as a product of individuals' circumstances, as well as unique cultural, socioeconomic, and familial situations. When policymakers ignore how and why parents make choices, they limit their ability to best serve the needs of diverse populations. By focusing on how parents and guardians choose schools for their children, how policies affect their decisions, and how these considerations are often overlooked in the conventional discourse about choice in education, we believe that policymakers can better ensure that educational policies benefit all children.

WHAT IS PARENTAL CHOICE IN EDUCATION?

If listening to the mainstream debate is your only source of information on parental choice, you would probably assume that parental choice is simply vouchers and charter schools, but parental choice in education is far more complex. Let us begin by considering choice within two broad categories: *inherent* and *public policy* choice.

Inherent Choice

Inherent choice is essentially a function of parental resources. Given sufficient time and money, parents can choose where and how their children learn. They can move to areas with better public schools, enroll their children at private schools, or devote their own time to homeschooling. Inherent choice is, of course, not a recent phenomenon and has historically been a function of privilege (Figure 2.1).

Public Policy Choice

Public policy choice is the result of a government's intentional expansion of educational choices for families. Such policies are a relatively new phenomenon, despite being rooted in almost three centuries of economic theory.

With the growth of universal education in the 18th and 19th centuries, the concept of choice in education quickly became an issue of debate, beginning with one of the forefathers of capitalist thought, Adam Smith. Smith argued that parents should be free to choose schools for their children, but they should also be prohibited from making unwise

Figure 2.1. Inherent Parental Choice in Education

Element	Simple Definition	Example
Mobility	As public schools may differ in quality between geographical locations, parents can move to districts with superior schools.	Parents living in a school district with underperforming schools can move the family to a district with higher performing schools.
Private schools	Parents can enroll children in parochial or other fee-charging private schools. Private schools are not obliged to admit students, and some are competitive. Some award scholarships to excellent students.	The most prestigious private schools in the United States have strict entry requirements and are extremely expensive.
Homeschooling	Parents can choose to educate children in their own home.	Parents in extremely rural areas or parents who are fundamentally unhappy with the schooling options available may choose to homeschool their children.

choices. He argued that education should be compulsory, and governments must ensure that all schools provide an education that benefits both the individual and the public. While an advocate of free choice, Smith also had moral reservations about the equity of a completely free-choice system of education could afford (Smith, 1776; West, 2005).

Public policy choice largely remained an object of philosophical debate rather than active implementation until the latter half of the 20th century. It was at this point that parental choice in education found its champion, Milton Friedman.

> We believe that the growing role that government has played in financing and administering schooling has led not only to enormous waste of taxpayers' money but also to a far poorer educational system than would have developed had voluntary cooperation continued to play a larger role. (Friedman & Friedman, 1980, p. 187)

Proponents of public policy choice present a theory with a certain beautiful simplicity to it. By improving parents' opportunities to choose, the best schools will grow and thrive while the worst schools will be replaced by better options. All students will benefit. Beginning with Friedman, economists have argued that the public provision of education functions as a monopoly. Immune to market pressures, public education systems have few incentives to improve educational outcomes. Choice, they argue, is the antidote. If public money follows parental choices, then schools would be subject to the same market forces that reward successful businesses and force failing businesses to close. Given that inherent choice is out of reach for many families, advocates view public policy choice as a means for all families to access choice and exert pressure on educational systems to improve. While the mechanisms vary, most public policy choice operates under this fundamental theory.

Friedman's ideas gained traction in the 1970s and 1980s as public policy choice became a hotly contested issue. In the United States, the famous *A Nation at Risk* report (1983) ignited support for public policy choice under the claim that public school systems were failing, and radical change was necessary. Similar reports were also released internationally, such as New Zealand's *Tomorrow's Schools* in 1988.

What does public policy choice look like when implemented? In Figure 2.2, we present a comparative summary of the most common mechanisms used by governments to expand parental choice in education.

The principles that underpin public policy choice in education are closely tied to various propositions of neoliberalism: transfer of control to the private sector, deregulation, decentralization, reduced government spending, and consumer choice as a mechanism to improve quality. In theory, public policy choice places pressure on a competitive system of schools such that all schools will eventually improve, and those that don't will close due to lack of demand. However, after several decades of implementation across the world, improved quality has not been a consistent result of public policy choice in education. While many countries have enjoyed some of the benefits predicted by neoliberal theories in education, public policy choice has also come with unexpected outcomes. We wondered whether, if traditional economic theory doesn't explain all the outcomes of parental choice in education, there are other theories that can.

BEYOND RATIONAL ACTOR THEORY: EXPLORATIONS OF CHOICE

Economists have driven the discussion of choice in education for the past half century. While we do not reject their theories outright, they left us with several key unanswered questions. We believe that not addressing these questions undermines the assumptions upon which public policy choice is founded:

Figure 2.2. Public Policy Choice in Education

Policy/ Strategy	Simple Definition	U.S. Examples	International Examples
Magnet schools	Competitive-entry public schools that focus on a specific discipline.	The School of Science and Engineering in the Dallas Independent School District requires applicants to take standardized tests for entry.	Chile has a similar program, with *Liceos de Excelencia* (public high schools of excellence) functioning within the public sector as examples of academic excellence.
Charter schools	Publicly funded (nonprofit or for-profit) schools to which parents can opt in. Charters have greater autonomy than public schools, as they do not have to follow the same regulatory framework. In return, they are supposed to be held accountable to the terms of their charter.	KIPP Academy is a large chain of charter schools operating in urban areas with low-performing public schools.	In Sweden, independent nonmunicipal schools receive the same per-child funding as public schools. They can be for-profit but cannot charge additional fees. This structure has existed in Sweden since the 1990s and currently serves about 25% of students (Åstrand, 2016).
Vouchers	Governments provide money to families who choose not to enroll their children in public schools. This money can only be used to fund education at accredited institutions. Vouchers may or may not cover the full cost of private schools.	Thirteen U.S. states have some form of publically funded school vouchers for qualifying students; for example, the Milwaukee Parental Choice Program (1990), the Ohio Educational Choice Scholarship Program (2005), and the Indiana Choice Scholarship Program (2011) (NCSL, 2016).	Since 1981, Chile has provided vouchers to fund student enrollment in privately managed school options. These schools historically have been regulated but permitted to make a profit, select students, and charge copayments. A law enacted in 2015 restricts these aspects of subsidized schools. Current figures indicate that 54% of Chilean students attend privately managed, subsidized schools under the voucher program (Chumacero et al., 2011).

Figure 2.2. Public Policy Choice in Education (*continued*)

Policy/ Strategy	Simple Definition	U.S. Examples	International Examples
Open enrollment	Parents can send their children to any public school without being limited by residence.	Under Title I of the No Child Left Behind Act in the United States, parents of children at underperforming public schools have the right to enroll their children in an adequately performing school within the district.	In the 1990s, New Zealand decentralized and dezoned its schools, permitting parents to choose to enroll their child in a nonlocal school. The system was modified in 2000 to require schools to accept children within their local zones, and it permits parents to apply for enrollment of their children in other schools when vacancies exist (Morphis, 2009).

1. In a world full of educational choices, how do parents choose?
2. Do all parents make decisions in the same way?
3. How and why do decisions differ across cultures, groups, and classes?

With this in mind, we came to a concluding question: "How does existing neoliberal theory approach choice, and how well does that approach fit the true diversity of human action?" Rather than providing answers to these questions, we hope to expand the dialogue around parental choice in education by merging the worlds of economics, psychology, and sociology.

In the late 19th century, philosopher John Stuart Mill popularized the concept of the *homo economicus*, the economically self-interested man originally described by Adam Smith in 1776. Mill's theory presumed that humans are monetarily driven and consider options rationally when making choices (Mill, 1836). Throughout the century, economists built their models on this assumption, culminating in the creation of *rational actor theory*, in which people are assumed to carefully assess information and account for future probable costs and benefits when making decisions.

Behavioral economics, and later identity economics, both arose to expand and to challenge traditional economics and rational actor theory. By shifting from an assumption of objective rationality and taking into account the complex psychological, cognitive, and emotional processes that shape individuals' choices, behavioral economics explores the factors that form people's preferences and perceptions of value (Kahneman & Tversky, 1979; Simon, 1955). Identity economics builds upon this framework, observing how conceptions of identity and cultural norms can work together to influence individuals' decisions (Akerlof & Kranton, 2011).

Nobel Prize–winning economist Douglass North further expanded the economics of choice through the framework of mental models (Denzau & North, 1994; North, 1992). He defines them as "pre-existing mental constructs through which actors understand the environment and solve the problems they confront" (North, 1990, p. 20). Individual and shared perceptions of the world and the way it functions form an overlap of values, attitudes, and beliefs that inform common-lived experiences and the intergenerational transmission of culture.

We found that these more complex theories of choice rarely enter the debate around parental choice in education. However, we believe they may offer insight and help us better understand how groups view and approach opportunities, responding to choice policies in divergent and sometimes seemingly irrational ways. They may help us to understand why unexpected results occur when public policy choice is implemented. These theories admittedly lack the appealing conceptual simplicity of the logic of rational actor theory that drives most public policy choice and does not imply a clear course of policy. However, we believe that public policy choice that ignores complex theories of decision making is destined to be ineffective at best and, in some cases, will exacerbate existing inequities or cause unexpected outcomes.

PARENTAL CHOICE ON THE WORLD STAGE

To best discuss the implications of parental choice in education, we have chosen to examine countries that fall across the spectrum of *inherent* and *public policy* choice (Figure 2.3). We look at Chile and Sweden, both of which embraced Friedman's ideas and expanded public policy choice, including the use of public money in the private sector. We also examine New Zealand, which experimented with expanding choice within the public sector but later scaled back some of those reforms. India and Finland are stark contrasts on both dimensions. In India, both high- and low-income parents take advantage of extensive

Figure 2.3. The Spectrum of Inherent and Public Policy Choice

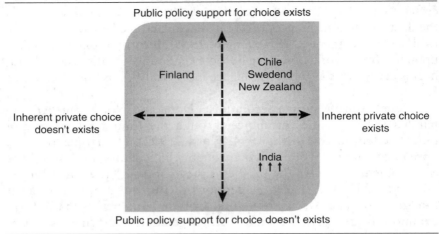

Public policy support for choice exists

Finland

Chile
Swedend
New Zealand

Inherent private choice
doesn't exists

Inherent private choice
exists

India
↑ ↑ ↑

Public policy support for choice doesn't exists

inherent choice, and the country is in the process of vastly expanding public policy choice in the private sector. In Finland, despite the existence of choice within the public system, parents infrequently exercise this option.

In each country, we begin with a description of the goals and the mechanisms of public policy choice and a brief overview of the current situation. We then describe both the outcomes expected by traditional economic theory and the unexpected outcomes that these theories did not predict or were not designed to explain. We hope you will consider whether some of these unexpected outcomes could have been avoided or mitigated if alternative theories of choice, for example behavioral economics, identity economics, and mental models, had been considered during policy development.

CHILE: Current population: 17.6 million. School-aged children: 3.9 million. Percentage of students attending public schools: 37%.

Policy Goals and Mechanisms. Parental choice in education has a long history in Chile, with private institutions existing alongside public schools since the 19th century (Ley 349: Libertad de Enseñanza, 1878). Radical school choice was implemented through vouchers in 1981, which resulted in privatization at many levels. Chilean parents can use these vouchers to choose between public and privately managed schools in what can best be described as a complex and deregulated market system (Chumacero et al., 2011; Kosunen & Carrasco, 2014, p. 4). Under these policies, Chile offers almost universal coverage through a diverse supply of schools (Chumacero et al., 2011).

Current Situation. Approximately 54% of students in Chile attend privately managed schools with vouchers, while another 8% attend unsubsidized, fully private schools, and only 37% attend public schools (Ministerio de Educación, 2016). Parents can exercise inherent choice through residential moves and selecting unsubsidized private schools. They can also access public policy choice with a wide range of schools supported by public finance. Privately managed schools have historically been regulated but have been permitted to make a profit, select students, and charge copayments. However, a new law (Ley de Inclusion, 2015), seeks to reduce system-wide inequities and places new restrictions on subsidized schools.

Expected Outcomes. Chile's policies resulted in a series of complex outcomes. They are generally considered to have led to increased school coverage, a slow but measurable improvement in academic outcomes, for example in Programme for International Student Assessment (PISA), and increased enrollments in tertiary education.

Unexpected Outcomes. Evidence also suggests that the reforms have exacerbated inequities, and parents use widely differing factors such as social signaling, convenience, word-of-mouth, and only occasionally test results to make educational school choices (Chumacero et al., 2011; Thieme & Treviño, 2011). The less-than-satisfying improvements in quality and increased socioeconomic stratification have resulted in civil unrest, with Chilean students protesting rising inequities.

SWEDEN: Current population: 9.8 million. School-aged children: 1.5 million. Percentage of students attending public schools: 75%.

Policy Goals and Mechanisms. Sweden was an early and radical adopter of school choice policies through the introduction of the *Free School* (friskola) model in the 1990s. These independent schools are essentially charter schools that receive the same amount of per-child funding as public schools. These schools were originally envisioned as offering alternative or specialized pedagogical profiles, but this has become diluted over time. They may be organized within different legal and administrative entities, for example, publicly listed companies, faith-based organizations, and cooperatives, but while they may be for-profit institutions, they may not charge additional fees (Åstrand, 2016).

Current Situation. Both inherent and public policy choices exist in Sweden, with parents making residential choices and selecting between private and public educational offerings for their children. Recent figures indicate that up to 25% of schools are charter schools, and as many as 50% of upper secondary schools are privately managed (The Swedish Institute, 2015). As decentralization and privatization permit less strict regulations, private schools tend to have fewer highly trained teachers and larger class sizes (Åstrand, 2016). As of 2016, an educational commission is convened in Sweden to propose education policies to address the criticisms of school choice policies and the pressing problem of a major teacher shortage within the system.

Expected Outcomes. Early evaluations indicated that success of the *Free School* model was aligned with neoliberal theory—decentralization, privatization, competition, and choice seemed to increase the system-wide efficiency and create the sensation that education was improving. Even today, in the midst of a critical reexamination, public policy choice is generally viewed positively. A large number of parents take advantage of the private educational choices offered by the *Free School* model.

Unexpected Outcomes. Sweden's steady decline on international educational assessments is not easily explained by traditional economic theories. In addition, several initially successful for-profit charter schools have suffered bankruptcy, which together with declining results has eroded confidence in the efficacy of the reforms (Åstrand, 2016). There are increasing concerns about the ability of choice to improve the quality of education, particularly as indicators usually associated with school quality, such as teacher qualifications and student-to-teacher ratio, are not particularly influential in parental educational decisions (Åstrand, 2016). On the labor side of education, widespread teacher dissatisfaction within the system resulted in a looming teacher shortage.

NEW ZEALAND: Current population: 4.5 million. School-aged children: 0.8 million. Percentage of students in public schools: 96%.

Policy Goals and Mechanisms. In 1991, New Zealand schools were dezoned, allowing parents to select a school without considering geographical areas that had originally been established to protect the right of families to send their children to local schools (Morphis, 2009). By expanding parental choice in the public sector and by decentralizing the management of schools, the government placed financial incentives on underperforming schools to improve. In 1995, the government introduced *deciles*, a socioeconomic classification system for schools, to help identify schools in need of additional funding. While not intended as such, the decile system became a signal of quality to parents, who removed their children from lower-decile schools in favor of higher-decile schools (Morphis, 2009). These schools became oversubscribed to the point that local residents were unable to enroll their children. The government responded with a quick succession of new laws that reinstated every child's right to attend their local school, with out-of-zone applicants only being accepted after local children (Pearce & Gordon, 2005). However, even with these changes, these policies increased socioeconomic segregation among schools (Heyneman, 2008).

Current Situation. School choice policies mostly have been unaltered since legislation in 2000 required schools to accept students from their local zone, allowing parental choice only when spaces exist in alternative schools. Education today in New Zealand is, therefore, a mix of public provision and parental choice. Parents can make residential decisions (inherent choice) or apply for limited spaces in schools outside of their residential areas (public policy choice).

Expected Outcomes. Despite some negative consequences, public policy choice is widely supported by parents and politicians alike. It appears that while there is little evidence of impact on educational quality, many parents enjoy the opportunity to exercise a limited form of public policy choice.

Unexpected Outcomes. New Zealand's reforms were designed to encourage excellent schools to expand and underperforming schools to improve or close. These reforms did not deliver on these promises. In addition, the reaction of parents to the decile ranking system and increased residential segregation have been unintended consequences of the public policy choice reforms.

INDIA: Current population: 1.3 billion. School-aged children: 360 million. Approximate number of out-of-school children: 17.7 million.

Policy Goals and Mechanisms. In comparison to the previous three cases, India's experiments with public policy choice are more recent. However, it represents the context with perhaps the greatest access to inherent choice, and if the Right to Education (RTE) Act is fully implemented as planned,

India may become the country with the largest public policy choice in the world. Wealthy parents have long enjoyed the privilege of selecting elite schools for their children, often within large urban cities. The emergence of low-fee private schools has increased inherent choice for historically underserved groups. Expanding on this phenomenon, under the RTE, private schools are required to reserve 25% of places for disadvantaged students attending with publically provided vouchers (Muralidharan & Sundararaman, 2015). However, there is intense resistance to the implementation of these policies, with parents fearing a decline in the quality of education at private schools.

Current Situation. It is estimated that between 25 and 50% of students now attend private schools, including low-fee unsubsidized schools, newly emerging voucher schools, and expensive, elite private schools (Joshua, 2014).

Expected Outcomes. Evidence from experiments undergird India's current expansion of public policy choice. Muralidharan and Sundararaman (2015) demonstrated that providing vouchers to a private school increased test scores slightly in comparison to public school counterparts and did not lead to negative spillover effects on students left in public school. Multiple other studies found convincing results of the cost efficiency of the Indian private education system.

Unexpected Outcomes. Localized experiments demonstrated the benefits that public policy choice might provide and have lent credence to traditional economic theories. However, there are concerns about its widespread implementation. Many continue to worry that choice will result in increased segregation. Others worry that increasing public policy choice may not improve education. For example, Srivastava (2008) found that many parents consider large classroom sizes an indicator of school quality. If such associations are not actually indicative of a superior education, then increased choice may not lead to improved quality.

FINLAND: Current population: 5.5 million. School-aged children: 0.9 million. Percentage of students attending public schools: 97%.

Policy Goals and Mechanisms. Contrary to popular belief, public policy choice does exist in the Finnish education system. Despite only 3% of schools being state-subsidized private schools, the Education Act of 1998 diversified schooling options and choice within the public system, while confirming that education must be provided without fees (Kosunen &

Carrasco, 2014; Seppänen et al., 2015). This public policy choice does not stem from a desire to foster competition to incentivize schools to improve. Rather, it is an effort to increase the availability of specialized educational opportunities. To prevent inequitable sorting, specialized schools cannot admit students by general test scores and may only assess aptitude in the specific specialization of the school, for example music or science and technology. Choice in Finland means that parents have the right to apply for a space for their child in a specialized school other than their local option, and municipalities are legally required to offer every child a space in a school that is within a safe and reasonable distance from their home (Seppänen et al., 2015).

Current Situation. Despite opportunities for educational choice in Finland, most parents do not exercise this option. Parental choice in education remains largely an urban phenomenon (Kosunen & Carrasco, 2014). Research indicates that "a high proportion of parents have a positive image of the Finnish educational system and think that most schools are 'good enough' throughout the country" (van Zanten in Seppänen et al., 2015, p. 5).

Expected Outcomes. In a country where all educational options are of a high quality, the ability for market forces to improve educational outcomes is limited. The opportunity cost of attending one school over another is low.

Unexpected Outcomes. Parents in Finland value all the educational options available to them and feel strongly about equality, rejecting the "tenets of market-oriented schooling or the ideology of competition and giftedness" (Kauka et al. in Seppänen et al., 2015, p. 43). This is possibly the clearest example of where traditional economic theory fails to explain human behavior.

ASKING THE RIGHT QUESTIONS, SERVING THE RIGHT PEOPLE

As can be seen in an international context, public policy choice impacts educational systems. Traditional economics and rational actor theory explain many of the outcomes of public policy choice and were influential in their design. However, other outcomes produced by these policy decisions are not well explained by these same theories. We pose the question again: Could some of these unexpected outcomes have been avoided, or at least mitigated, through the use of more recent economic theories that holistically consider human behavior?

Public policy choice, in its many forms, is neither the savior nor the destroyer of education. We believe that a more nuanced view of choice that expands beyond conventional economic wisdom must be adopted by policymakers. The future of school choice will no doubt be one of compromise (Heyneman, 2008). Policies that are formed considering behavioral economics, as Jabbar (2011) describes, "usually retain aspects of consumer choice and the market. They tend to have bipartisan appeal, and because they start from realistic assumptions about human behavior, these policies may be more likely to elicit the intended behavioral responses."

Traditional economic theory and the rational actor model of choice cannot explain all school choice outcomes. They were never intended to account for the complexities of how people, in reality, act. However, economics has evolved to incorporate analyses of observed human behavior on both the individual and the societal level; policy should too. It is essential that policymakers consider the potentially divergent behavioral nuances of individuals and design policies that will equitably and successfully serve our diverse populations. How could our educational systems be improved if policymakers embraced a more nuanced view of choice?

REFERENCES

Akerlof, G., & Kranton, R. (2011). *Identity economics: How our identities shape our work, wages and well-being.* Princeton, NJ: Princeton University Press.

Åstrand, B. (2016). From citizens to consumers: The transformation of democratic ideals into school markets in Sweden. In F. Adamson, B. Åstrand, & L. Darling-Hammond (Eds.), *Global education reform: How privatization and public investment influence education outcomes* (pp. 73–109). New York, NY: Taylor & Francis.

Chumacero, R., Gomez, D., & Paredes, R. (2011). I would walk 500 miles (if it paid): Vouchers and school choice in Chile. *Economics of Education Review, 30*(5), 1103–1114. doi:10.1016/j.econedurev.2011.05.015

Denzau, A., & North, D. (1994). Shared mental models: Ideologies and institutions. *Kyklos, 47,* 3–31.

Friedman, M., & Friedman, R. (1980). *Free to choose: A personal statement.* New York, NY: Harcourt Brace Jovanovich.

Heyneman, S. (2008). International perspectives on school choice. In M. Berends, M. Springer, D. Ballou, & H. Walberg (Eds.), *Handbook of research on school choice* (pp. 79–96). Mahwah, NJ: Lawrence Erlbaum Publishers.

Jabbar, H. (2011). The behavioral economics of education. *Educational Researcher, 40*(9), 446–453.

Joshua, A. (2014, January 16). Over a quarter of enrollments in rural India are in private schools. *The Hindu.* Retrieved from http://www.thehindu.com/

Kahneman, D., & Tversky, A. (1979). Prospect theory: An analysis of decision under risk. *Econometrica, 47*(2), 263–292.

Kosunen, S., & Carrasco, A. (2014). Parental preferences in school choice: Comparing reputational hierarchies of schools in Chile and Finland. *Compare: A Journal of Comparative and International Education,* 1–22. doi:10.1080/0305 7925.2013.861700

Mill, J. (1836). On the definition of political economy, and on the method of investigation proper to it. In *Essays on Some Unsettled Questions of Political Economy,* 2nd ed. London, UK: Longmans, Green, Reader, & Dyer, 1874.

Ministerio de Educación. (2016). *Centro de estudios.* Retrieved from http://centroestudios.mineduc.cl/index.php?t=96

Morphis, E. (2009). *New Zealand school reform.* Washington, DC. Retrieved from http://www.ncspe.org

Muralidharan, K., & Sundararaman, V. (2015). The aggregate effect of school choice: evidence from a two-stage experiment in India. *NBER Working Paper Series, Sep 2013,* 19441.

National Conference of State Legislatures. (2016). *School voucher laws: State-by-state comparison.* Retrieved from http://www.ncsl.org/research/education/voucher-law-comparison.aspx

North, D. (1990). *Institutions, institutional change and economic performance.* Cambridge, UK: Cambridge University Press.

North, D. (1992). Institutions and economic theory. *American Economist (Spring 1992),* 3–6.

Pearce, D., & Gordon, L. (2005). In the zone: New Zealand's legislation for a system of school choice and its effects. *London Review of Education, 3*(2), 145–157. doi:10.1080/14748460500163955

Seppänen, P., Carrasco, A., Kalalahti, M., Rinne, R., & Simola, H. (Eds.). *Contrasting dynamics in education politics of extremes: School choice in Chile and Finland* (pp. 3–28). Rotterdam, The Netherlands: Sense Publishers.

Simon, H. (1955). A behavioral model of rational choice. *Quarterly Journal of Economics, 69*(1), 99–118.

Smith, A. (1776). *The wealth of nations, books I–III.* New York, NY: Penguin Classics, 1986.

Srivastava, P. (2008). School choice in India: disadvantaged groups and low-fee private schools. In M. Forsey, S. Davies, & G. Walford (Eds.), *The globalisation of school choice* (pp. 185–208). Oxford, UK: Symposium Books.

The Swedish Institute. (2015). Education in Sweden. Retrieved April 4, 2016, from https://sweden.se/society/education-in-sweden/

Thieme, C., & Treviño, E. (2011). School choice and market imperfections: Evidence from Chile. *Education and Urban Society, 45*(6), 635–657. doi:10.1177/0013124511413387

West, E. (2005). Adam Smith's proposal on public education. *Economic Affairs,* (March).

CHAPTER 3

What Is the Right Answer to the Standardized Testing Question?

Momar Dieng, Elaine Koh, & Lauren Marston

According to W. James Popham, former president of the American Educational Research Association, a *standardized test* is "any test that is administered, scored, and interpreted in a standard, predetermined manner" (Popham, 2005). Standardized tests have been a part of American education since the mid-1800s, but their use in the United States skyrocketed after the No Child Left Behind Act (NCLB) passed in 2002, mandating annual testing of 3rd to 8th grades in public schools in reading and mathematics in all 50 states. Since then, the performance of U.S. students has plummeted relative to other developed countries in international benchmarking tests in mathematics, science, and reading ("Standardized Tests," 2016). This fact demonstrates that standardized testing has not improved student achievement in the United States as many of the proponents of the NCLB expected. In fact, on May 26, 2011, the National Research Council reported that there is no evidence that test-based incentive programs are working and stated that "despite using them for several decades, policymakers and educators do not yet know how to use test-based incentives to consistently generate positive effects on achievement and to improve education" (Hout & Elliott, 2011).

A lack of improvement in student achievement, one of the primary goals of mandating standardized testing in 2002, prompts consideration as to what benefits standardized testing actually offers and begs the question: Do those benefits outweigh the negative effects? In an attempt to begin to address that question, we invite you to answer the following:

Which of the following is true about standardized testing?

a. Instruction time is being consumed by monotonous test preparation.
b. Teacher promotions and salaries should be given according to their students' performance on standardized tests.
c. Teachers should teach to the tests in order to improve student performance.
d. Standardized testing causes severe stress in students.

What was your answer?
Congratulations, you have just failed your first test!

There is no one right answer to the standardized testing question, and, therefore, it's no surprise that you failed your first test. The above-mentioned options are just a few of the ways that standardized testing has been misused in the United States. It is our belief that standardized testing, if done well or SMARTly, can have tremendous benefits for an education system as a diagnostic and improvement tool. However, if not done well, standardized testing can have negative effect on students, teachers, schools, and districts.

THERE IS A SMART WAY TO DO THIS

Education systems around the world design and implement standardized testing in a variety of ways. In the following sections, we use Singapore and Finland as illustrative case studies to demonstrate how standardized testing can be used to strengthen teaching and learning—and improve student performance overall. We analyze our case studies through the lens of the SMART framework, which we suggest as a useful protocol and checklist of the features of a productive standardized testing strategy.

The SMART framework appeared in the early 1980s in business circles as a way to systematize goal-setting and the process to plan for the attainment of those goals (Doran, 1981). It has since found applications in virtually every area of business and organizational management, and variants of it have been used in designing and evaluating public policies. It provides a concise way to articulate the tenets we believe make for an effective use of educational assessment. The application is not far-fetched, insofar as there is one thing all sides in the heated assessment debate agree on: assessments are critical for quality assurance. In that sense, quality assurance can be seen as the larger concern around which consensus is possible. According to the American Society for Quality, *quality assurance* comprises administrative and procedural activities implemented in a quality system so that requirements and goals for a product, service, or activity will be fulfilled. The SMART framework consist of five principles that processes and policies follow (Figure 3.1).

Specific

The first tenet of SMART testing is to be *specific*, which means targeting a specific area for improvement and defining a specific objective before administering tests. Finland is one of the best examples of strict adherence to this principle of parsimonious testing. Finnish students undergo only two

Figure 3.1. SMART Framework

S pecific	✓ Targets a specific area for im provement ✓ Serves a specific purpose
M easurable	✓ Provides a quantifiable indicator of progresss/growth
A ttainable	✓ Results can be realistically achieved, given existing resources
R elevant	✓ Aligned with curriculum objectives and broader educational goals
T imely	✓ Tests administered in a timely fashion during the child's learning journey ✓ Results are made available in a timely manner.

Adapted from Doran (1981)

comprehensive standardized tests: one at the end of middle school and one at the end of high school (Hendrickson, 2012). Sahlberg (2015) attributes Finland's consistent lead on international assessments, such as the Programme for International Student Assessment (PISA), to this practice of testing only when there is a specific academic purpose versus for arbitrary accountability. Compare this to frequent high-stakes testing that has become a global trend in education, though it has not been proven to meaningfully increase student performance and does not have a specific purpose beyond ceremonious rigor. By contrast, Finland favors an assessment strategy that is encouraging and supportive by nature (Finnish National Board of Education, 2010).

Another high-performing system that is quite different from Finland in terms of frequency of high-stakes testing is Singapore. In Singapore, all students of the particular age cohort take the standardized test. This happens three times in the span of K–12 education. Singapore adopts a range of assessment tools for different purposes; high-stakes exams are specifically meant for student sorting, which in turn allows for differentiated instruction in the various tracks and schools, and provide policymakers with descriptive information about how well students are performing (Heng, 2014). Other purposes for offering teachers' diagnostic information to shape instruction, retrospectively and prospectively, are fulfilled with other assessment tools such as formative assessment during the course of the school year, summative midyear/year-end examinations, and holistic assessment, a form of performance assessment (Ng, 2015). These tests are not without their downsides. First, due to the high stakes accorded to the very few number of standardized tests, these exams are a huge source of stress and anxiety for students, parents, and teachers (Heng, 2013; Ng, 2015). Further, even for the high-stakes assessment, the domain measured is very narrow, given the pen-and-paper nature of the exams (Ong, 2016). These instruments use an overly narrow yardstick to measure student merit, focusing only on academic achievement (Tan, 2016). To this end, Singapore seeks to supplement information on student performance afforded by these assessments with other modes of assessment to provide a more comprehensive picture of a child's ability and progress. It also does not do justice to the holistic nature of the Singapore education system, where the total curriculum comprises both academic and nonacademic curriculum to nurture the whole child.

Measurable

The second tenet of SMART testing is that of making the effects of testing *measurable*, where the test can provide a quantifiable indicator of student progress. In Finland, instead of an intense focus on test preparation, educational policy guides administrators and teachers to target the curricular content and behaviors that drive learning, which then translate to measurable differences when students are tested. This plays out in three key ways. One, Finnish students receive instruction and support to develop excellent study skills. Two, teachers give frequent feedback, showing students where and how to improve. They are also taught how to analyze their own performance. In addition, their parents are kept abreast of their academic achievements and areas for improvement. Three, students' understanding of curriculum content is monitored year-round and is part of the systematic feedback loop in class. This combination of instilling solid academic habits in students, guiding teachers to provide frequent feedback to both students and parents, and measuring curricular progress constantly creates a powerful trifecta that results in high student achievement in core subjects as well as on standardized tests.

In the case for Singapore, these high-stakes tests set clear standards, provide an objective source of information for school sorting, for monitoring and tracking of performance and progress, and allow for comparability of results across cohorts. These exams provide a standardized measure of progression and achievement, and they ensure accountability across the system to uphold rigorous standards. In fact, this is one of the reasons public examinations were started in Singapore. It also provides an objective way of determining entry into the next level of education. Any other assessment mode that bears such high stakes should be deemed by parents and the public as a fair and transparent one. Nonetheless, not all things that are measurable are important; not all important things can be measured (Koretz, 2008; Ng, 2015). Instances of the latter include passion for lifelong learning, leadership competencies, the ability to work collaboratively in teams, and managing ambiguity. In administering high-stakes standardized tests, a system ought to recognize the limitations of what such tests cannot measure and supplement with other modes of assessment (Koretz, 2008). It is for this reason that the Ministry of Education, Singapore, has been steadily rolling out holistic assessment to all primary schools since 2009. Instead of a singular, heavy emphasis on year-end summative, pen-and-paper examinations, *holistic assessment* involves schools using a range of assessment modes and bite-sized forms of formative assessment for richer feedback on learning. The scope and the frequency of assessment are designed to ensure it is age-appropriate and manageable, with a tight nexus between curriculum, assessment, and pedagogy. Holistic assessment helps to build confidence towards learning in students and offers teachers diagnostic information to tailor and customize their instruction for better learning (Fu, 2010). Comprehensive feedback is shared regularly with the student and the parents to inform parents how their child is growing holistically—in academic learning, social-emotionally, in values and character, and how the child can be better in every way. Hence, parents are better able to partner with teachers and schools to support the holistic development of each child (Heng, 2013). Holistic assessment, therefore, is Singapore's approach to harnessing the full potential of assessment to enhance teaching and learning, beyond high-stakes standardized testing and other forms of summative assessment.

Attainable

The third facet of a SMART test is that it should offer what results can be *realistically achieved*, given available resources. In order to do this, it should be approached within the framework of formative assessment, which can be defined as "all those activities undertaken by teachers, and/or by their students, which provide information to be used as feedback to modify the teaching and learning activities in which they are engaged" (Black & Wiliam, 1998; Hendrickson, 2012). In Finland, the purpose of assessment is to guide and encourage studying and self-assessment skills. Assessment measures a combination of educational progress, work skills, and behavior (Finnish National Board of Education, 2010). Classroom assessment practices in Finland allow teachers to evaluate and change instruction based on student needs because they focus on improving instruction and learning, evaluating student progress, and providing feedback for students to understand their own thinking (Hendrickson, 2012).

    To ensure achievability, all standardized exams in Singapore are closely aligned with the national curriculum. Teachers have access to learning and teaching materials, professional development resources, and opportunities that are tailored to deepen pedagogy, curriculum, and assessment of national curriculum. All citizens have to take the standardized exam before leaving primary school—mandatory participation allows for comparison of standards and performance to facilitate school sorting. Unfortunately, due to the high stakes for the individual child, there is a pervasive problem of inappropriate test preparation (Koretz, 2008) in Singapore. More affluent parents are able to confer more advantages and resources to their children, proliferating a private tuition arms race that widens the opportunity and achievement gap in Singapore (Davie, 2015; Tan, 2016). Given this increasingly unleveled playing field, resources available to different groups of students could vary depending on their socioeconomic statuses; therefore, what is achievable within those enabling or limiting circumstances is also variable (Teng, 2015). Teachers play a critical role in providing quality assessment and learning for our children. To support the nationwide implementation of holistic assessment, the Singapore Ministry of Education also developed materials, assessment exemplars, rubrics, and other professional development resources to support schools in their execution and sharing of the best practices. There are professional development platforms that focus on these specific areas to help teachers hone their skills (Fu, 2010).

Relevant

The fourth facet of SMART testing is a test that is *relevant*—aligned with curriculum objectives and broader educational goals. Kasanen, Raty, and Snellman (2003) explain how Finnish teachers frequently use tests and test-like situations in primary schools but avoid presenting the situations as tests. Numerical grading is not used in these instances, but they are often scored or marked with a scale of very good to needs practice. The results are often not provided to students or parents but are used by teachers for planning. The only genuine test situations are presented in the second half of the school year, and they provide a summative overview of what has been learned. As a result, Finnish students see test situations as learning experiences rather than assessments (Hendrickson, 2012).

In Singapore, standardized tests have been useful in ensuring high standards and rigor for literacy and numeracy. However, many skills and competencies that are increasingly valued today are not easily measurable. This speaks to the need to diversify the modes of assessment to monitor and measure other domains of students' growth, merit, and achievement to keep assessment realistic and relevant (Ng, 2015). Holistic assessment is one way of doing so. Above all, to deliver a relevant, high-quality education that can realistically prepare our children for the future, Singapore needs to address the larger question of how to prioritize and streamline in order to meet the various goals of education (Ng, 2015).

Timely

The final facet of SMART testing is that it is *timely*; tests are not just administered in a timely fashion during the child's learning journey, but results are made available in a timely manner. Timeliness is an important feature of assessments, one that ensures that grades convey more than mere scores and "communicate to the students what the score means and how they can improve their process" (Kulm, 1994). The Finnish National Board of Education (2004) encourages assessment that helps students become aware of their thinking as well as their progress through the curriculum. Student self-assessment is also a critical skill for Finnish students to develop (Hendrickson, 2012), and this can only be done when the assessment tightly follows the arc of learning. In Singapore, the frequency of administering standardized exams is sparing and judicious—one set before each graduation from a key stage of the learning journey: the end of primary education (grade 6), the end of secondary education (grade 10), and the end of junior college education (grade 12).

Results from standardized tests are released in a timely manner, within 3 months, to be used for posting of students' grades. Given the targeted purpose of high-stakes standardized exams in Singapore, these results are not meant to be fed into a feedback loop to adjust instruction. Such a purpose is served by other forms of ongoing assessment (assessment for learning). Rather, sorting students into various tracks and schools allows for customization and differentiated instruction to then take place at the next stage of their education journey. In the case of holistic assessment, teachers regularly share with parents both qualitative and quantitative feedback on the various aspects of student development (Heng, 2013; Fu, 2010).

THERE IS NO ONE RIGHT ANSWER TO THE QUESTION OF STANDARDIZED TESTING

Standardized testing, if done well or SMARTly, can have tremendous benefits for an education system, for example, as a diagnostic and improvement tool. However, the opposite is also true. If not done well, it can have little to no impact on student performance while coming at a high cost, both literally and figuratively, to students, teachers, schools, districts, and overall achievement.

As reflected in how vastly different standardized testing systems in Finland and Singapore revolve around the principles of testing encapsulated in the SMART framework, it is evident that there is no one right answer to the question of standardized testing. Rather, we propose that instead of attempting to find and/or design a one-size-fits-all model, various countries and systems should learn from others that do standardized testing well, taking into consideration the unique profile and needs of their own context. Once this is done, we recommend applying the SMART framework to their identified contexts, so as to reap the benefits that standardized testing has to offer while mitigating the associated costs. In international comparative studies, it is often said that we do not scale the formula or the template, but rather the principles—to internalize and apply it in each of our unique contexts. Metaphorically, we do not catch the same song but rather dance to the same beat. Extending this analogy, the SMART framework offered here is the beat or the rhythm. In working out how this beat would best play out in our unique contexts, we write our own music.

The way Singapore and Finland have successfully implemented testing to strengthen their education systems in diverse contexts can be contrasted to the U.S. model and the surrounding controversy.

THE HISTORY OF MODERN STANDARDIZED TESTING IN THE USA

In 1989, President George H.W. Bush proposed the America 2000 plan, which aimed to achieve the world's best math and science test scores by the turn of the century ("Standardized Tests," 2016). In 1994, President Clinton ushered in Goals 2000 to establish a framework in which to identify world-class academic standards and measure student progress on those standards. On January 8, 2002, the No Child Left Behind Act (NCLB) passed with bipartisan support and was signed into law by President George W. Bush. Annual testing in reading and mathematics, and later in science, for grades 3 through 8 and 10 was mandated as a part of this legislation (Hout & Elliott, 2011). Schools were held to higher standards and more specifically, to their adequate yearly progress (AYP). If they did not make sufficient progress, they faced sanctions and the possibility of being taken over by the state or closed ("Standardized Tests," 2016).

Later, President Barack Obama signed the American Recovery and Reinvestment Act (ARRA) of 2009, historic legislation designed to stimulate the economy, support job creation, and invest in critical sectors, including education, into law (U.S. Department of Education, 2009). The ARRA provides $4.35 billion for the Race to the Top Program Fund and invited states to compete for the extra funding based on the strength of their student test scores ("Standardized Tests," 2016). On March 13, 2010, Obama proposed an overhaul of NCLB, promising further incentives to states if they develop improved assessments tied more closely to state standards and emphasizing other indicators such as pupil attendance, graduation rates, and learning climate in addition to test scores ("Standardized Tests", 2016). However, it was not actually overhauled until December 2015 when Every Student Succeeds Act (ESSA) became effective.

STANDARDIZED TESTING IN THE UNITED STATES TODAY

No Child Left Behind (NCLB) encouraged the use of high-stakes testing to motivate and incentivize educators to improve their schools, teachers, and ultimately their student achievement (Morin, 2016). It included attaching rewards and punishments to test scores, with the reasoning being that school districts and administrators would make tough choices and put in the necessary effort to improve the educational outcomes for the students in their charge (Morin, 2016). As such, high-stakes achievement standardized tests carry important consequences for students, teachers, and schools (Morin, 2016). Some of these consequences include, but are not limited to, extra pressure on students and teachers, student retention, school closure, and teacher ratings based on student performance (Kolodner, 2011). In addition, the promotion of such tests resulted in a number of other negative effects on the U.S. education system, including but not limited to teaching to the test, loss of instructional time, and frequency of testing.

Teaching to the Test

Teaching to the test is being said to replace good teaching practices with drill 'n' kill rote learning ("Standardized Tests," 2016), forcing students to memorize (drill) and narrowing the use of creativity and critical thinking skills in the classroom (kill). Such teaching in the classroom can hamper students' joy in learning and teachers' passion in teaching. In fact, "a five-year University of Maryland study completed in 2007 found the pressure teachers were feeling to 'teach to the test' since NCLB was leading to declines in teaching higher-order thinking, in the amount of time spent on complex assignments, and in the actual amount of high cognitive content in the curriculum." ("Standardized Tests," 2016).

Loss of Instructional Time

Another argument against standardized testing is the number of hours devoted to test preparation, including but not limited to numerous hours and periods being used solely for test prep, as well as students and teachers coming in over vacation and/or taking test preparation home for vacations (Kolodner, 2011).

Frequency of Testing

A new Council of the Great City Schools study found that "in the United States, a typical student takes 112 mandated standardized tests between pre-kindergarten classes and 12th grade (Layton, 2015). The report also found that the heaviest testing load falls on the nation's eighth graders, who spend an average of 25.3 hours during the school year taking standardized tests, and that testing affects even the youngest students, with the average pre-K class given 4.1 standardized tests (Layton, 2015).

STANDARDIZED TESTING OPPOSITION IN THE UNITED STATES—A GAME CHANGER?

New standardized testing policies in the United States have produced the largest uprising against high-stakes testing in U.S. history (Hagopian, 2015). Students have walked out of tests in cities and states including Portland, Chicago, Colorado, and New Mexico, and teachers in others such as Seattle and New York City have refused to administer the tests (Hagopian, 2015). Additionally, the parent movement for their children to opt out of tests has exploded into a mass social movement, including 60,000 families in Washington state and more than 200,000 families in New York state (Hagopian, 2015).

Seemingly, these uprisings quickly caused President Obama to have a change of heart. In a surprising turn of events, President Obama announced that unnecessary testing is consuming too much instructional time and creating undue stress for educators and students (Hagopian, 2015). It seemed that the opposition to standardized testing from students, teachers, parents, and others has finally been heard, as President Obama expressed his regret in trying to reduce the intellectual and emotional process of teaching and learning to a single score, one that would be used to close schools, fire teachers and, deny a student's promotion or graduation (Hagopian, 2015). While President Obama has demonstrated commitment to reshape standardized testing in the United States, actual change remains to be seen.

Thinking about the evolution of standardized testing in the United States, we see that the system went from less to more, even to mandating tests and making high-stakes decisions as a result of them. Given this history and the resulting consequences and decision to reduce testing once more, we ask readers to envision what the SMART framework for standardized testing might look in the United States, in your school, in your district, and in your state. What should the future of standardized testing look like in the United States if done SMARTly? Remember, there is no one right answer to that question.

REFERENCES

Black, P., & Wiliam, D. (1998). Assessment and classroom learning. *Assessment in Education, 5*(1), 7–74.

Davie, S. (2015). *Tuition has become an educational arms race.* Retrieved from http://www.straitstimes.com/opinion/tuition-has-become-an-educational-arms-race

Doran, G. T. (1981). There's a S.M.A.R.T. way to write management's goals and objectives. *Management Review, 22*(11), 35–36.

Finnish National Board of Education. (2004). *National core curriculum for basic education 2004.* Retrieved from http://www.oph.fi/english/publications/2009/national_core_curricula_for_basic_education

Finnish National Board of Education. (2010). *Education.* Retrieved from http://www.oph.fi/english/education

Fu, G. (2010). *Speech by Ms. Grace Fu, Senior Minister of State, Ministry of National Development and Ministry of Education, at the PERI Holistic Assessment Seminar 2010 on Tuesday 13 July 2010.* Retrieved from https://www.moe.gov.sg/news/speeches/speech-by-ms-grace-fu--senior-minister-of-state--ministry-of-national-development-and-ministry-of-education--at-the-peri-holistic-assessment-seminar-2010-on-tuesday--13-july-2010-at-900-am-at-agora-hall--republic-polytechnic

Hagopian, J. (2015). *Obama regrets "taking the joy out of teaching and learning" with too much testing.* Retrieved from http://www.commondreams.org/views/2015/10/30/obama-regrets-taking-joy-out-teaching-and-learning-too-much-testing

Hendrickson, K. A. (2012). Assessment in Finland: A scholarly reflection on one country's use of formative, summative, and evaluative practices. *Mid-Western Educational Researcher, 25,* 33–43.

Heng, S. K. (2013). *Keynote address by the minister for education at the Ministry of Education Work Plan Seminar 2013.* Retrieved from https://www.moe.gov.sg/news/speeches/keynote-address-by-mr-heng-swee-keat--minister-for-education--at-the-ministry-of-education-work-plan-seminar-2013--on-wednesday--25-september-2013-at-915am-at-ngee-ann-polytechnic-convention-centre

Heng, S. K. (2014). *FY 2014 Committee of Supply Debate: First reply by Mr. Heng Swee Keat, minister for education: Bringing out the best in every child.* Retrieved from https://www.moe.gov.sg/news/speeches/fy-2014-committee-of-supply-debate--1st-reply-by-mr-heng-swee-keat--minister-for-education--bringing-out-the-best-in-every-child

Hout, M., & Elliott, S. (2011). *Incentives and test-based accountability in education.* http://doi.org/10.1080/0969594X.2013.877873

Kasanen, K., Raty, H., & Snellman, L. (2003). Learning the class test. *European Journal of Psychology of Education, 17*(1), 43–58.

Kolodner, M. (2011). *Students, teachers sweating tests.* Retrieved from http://www.nydailynews.com/new-york/education/students-teachers-sweating-high-stakes-tests-parents-rebel-constant-prep-article-1.140304

Koretz, D. (2008). What test scores tell us about American kids. In D. Koretz, *Measuring up: What educational testing really tells us* (pp. 77, 81–83). Cambridge, MA: Harvard University Press.

Kulm, G. (1994). *Mathematics assessment: What works in the classroom.* San Francisco, CA: Jossey-Bass.

Layton, L. (2015). *Study says standardized testing is overwhelming nation's public schools.* Retrieved from https://www.washingtonpost.com/local/education/study-says-standardized-testing-is-overwhelming-nations-public-schools/2015/10/24/8a22092c-79ae-11e5-a958-d889faf561dc_story.html

Morin, A. (2016). *What is high-stakes testing?* Retrieved from http://childparenting.about.com/od/schoollearning/a/high-stakes-tests-definition.htm

Ng, J. Y. (2015). *School content being cut to focus on critical learning.* Retrieved from http://www.todayonline.com/singapore/greater-emphasis-knowledge-application-coming-years-heng?singlepage=true

Ong, Y. K. (2016). *Speech by Mr. Ong Ye Kung, acting minister for education (higher education and skills), at debate of president's address, 25 Jan 2016, Parliament.* Retrieved from https://www.moe.gov.sg/news/speeches/speech-by-mr-ong-ye-kung--acting-minister-for-education-higher-education-and-skills--at-debate-of-presidents-address--25-jan-2016--parliament

Popham, W. J. (2005). *Standardized testing fails the exam.* Retrieved from http://www.edutopia.org/standardized-testing-evaluation-reform

Sahlberg, P. (2015). *Finnish lessons 2.0: What can the world learn from educational change in Finland.* New York, NY: Teachers College Press.

Standardized tests--ProCon.org. (2016). Retrieved from http://standardizedtests.procon.org/view.resource.php?resourceID=006521

Tan, K. B. E. (2016). *Going beyond exams in educating a nation.* Retrieved from http://m.todayonline.com/daily-focus/education/going-beyond-exams-educating-nation

Teng, A. (2015). *Starting from pre-school, parents sending kids for classes in race to keep up with peers.* Retrieved from http://www.straitstimes.com/singapore/education/starting-from-pre-school-parents-sending-kids-for-classes-in-race-to-keep-up

U.S. Department of Education. (2009). *Race to the top program: Executive summary.* Washington, DC: Author.

CHAPTER 4

Can Anyone Teach?

Fairuz Alia Jamaluddin, Lauren Owen, and Elyse Postlewaite

> At the start of my second year of teaching, I looked around the sparse library at the faces in our opening staff meeting. It seemed that every opening of the door brought in a new teacher accompanied by a blast of North Carolina heat to remind us of the oven-like August weather outside. Inside, the dilapidated air conditioner attempted to dispel both the heat and awkwardness of new acquaintances.
>
> Somewhere between the past spring and the beginning of that academic year, the school had lost approximately a quarter of its faculty, including two administrators and what seemed like a teacher in every department. Some vacancies had not yet been filled, and long-term substitutes would begin the school year.
>
> —Lauren Owen

The rush this district felt to find teachers resembled the challenge many schools across the globe face. Reaching universal access to education by 2015 had become an expected outcome due to the adoption of the Millennium Development Goals in 2000, which set expectations for solving global challenges such as universal primary education and HIV/AIDS. As a result, primary education enrollment increased from 83 to 91% in developing countries (United Nations, 2015).

With this increase in enrollment also came the need for more teachers. Governments and private enterprises have gone to great lengths to introduce new methods for recruiting, preparing, and equipping teachers to instruct in classrooms—from government-approved alternative

Hard Questions on Global Educational Change: Policies, Practices, and the Future of Education, edited by Pasi Sahlberg, Jonathan Hasak, Vanessa Rodriguez, and Associates. Copyright © 2017 by Teachers College, Columbia University. All rights reserved. Prior to photocopying items for classroom use, please contact the Copyright Clearance Center, Customer Service, 222 Rosewood Dr., Danvers, MA 01923, USA, www.copyright.com.

certification programs to school leadership pipelines such as *Teach for All* and *Bridge International Academies'* scripted content.

The presence of such varied programs calls into question what it means to teach in a formal educational setting and necessitates that education reformers answer the question: "Can anyone teach?" Is it sufficient to place a warm body in front of a group of students? If not, what must a teacher learn before he or she is fully equipped to teach, and how should a teacher education program—whether 4 weeks or 4 years—teach? What characteristics should a prospective teacher, someone entering into an instructional program to become a teacher, possess prior to beginning a program?

Our initial conversations around this question, as three educators from distinct backgrounds (one with a psychology background, one having done refugee education work, and one both a traditionally trained teacher and Teach for America alumna), pitted us against each other. We held three different positions—one with the view that a teacher needed to complete very specific preparation and develop traits, one arguing that anyone can teach, and another pushing for a contextualized view of teaching.

As we reviewed literature surrounding programs that prepare prospective teachers to enter a classroom, we found that they focused on formal schooling. The nature of entry requirements across these teacher education programs (TEPs) indicated that not everyone can teach. Individuals possess personal characteristics that we describe as relatively immutable, innate attributes that they are born with, which lead them to self-select into the teaching profession. These characteristics are apparent in programs requiring fewer teacher-specific credentials, such as Teach for America (TFA), as well as those with more rigorous credentialing requirements, such as Finland, Canada, and Singapore. TFA was not designed to act as a teacher education program. We explain our reasons for including it in a chapter on teacher education programs later in the chapter.

Though characteristics determine entry into a TEP, prospective teachers still require classroom preparation, a responsibility left to TEPs. However, characteristics and TEPs on their own or in tandem are not sufficient to declare a prospective teacher prepared for the classroom. This is in part due to the fact that a TEP only promotes teacher growth within the time confines of the program, and teaching is a skill as opposed to a set of characteristics (Rodriguez & Fitzpatrick, 2014). Given this, we saw a general lack of acknowledgement on the part of TEPs of the long-term growth process in which a teacher engages. This process occurs both during teacher education and after entering the classroom, and it is a developmental process. We refer to this concept of a developmental process as *teaching theory*. Without understanding this process, it is impossible to understand a teacher's development throughout his or her career. We define *teacher development* as the long-term growth process a teacher engages in after entering the classroom.

Therefore, for us to answer the question "Can anyone teach?", we must consider TEPs within the context of teaching theory. While we did not conduct the type of research to propose a teaching theory, we believe teaching theory is necessarily developmental and continue to make that assumption in this chapter when we refer to teaching theory. Since TEPs do play the most obvious role in beginning teacher development, we examine four of the internationally best-known TEPs: Teach for America, Montessori, and the TEPs of Finland and Singapore. After exploring the manner by which each program engages its teacher candidates with learning theory, content knowledge, pedagogical application, and practicum, we then seek to place these TEPs in the broader picture of teacher development. In doing so, we see the absence of a widely understood teaching theory—the trajectory of a teacher similar to learning theory. By understanding teaching theory, TEPs can better tailor their instruction to supporting long-term teacher growth and set teachers on a path to long-term growth.

TEACHER EDUCATION PROGRAMS: AN OVERVIEW

Teach for America, Montessori, Finland, and Singapore represent some of the most widely known teacher education programs (TEPs) around the world. We chose to focus on these programs because of the diversity they represent. However, it was difficult to find common ground between these TEPs to allow for a cohesive discussion of the programs. We, therefore, developed a format through which to compare them. Figure 4.1 summarizes these differences across the TEPs we chose to highlight.

First, each program bases its preparation on one or more *learning theories*, which we define as an understanding of how students acquire and build new knowledge. Throughout this chapter, we use the word *student* to refer to children in K–12 education whom prospective teachers will instruct, and it does not refer to pre-service or prospective teachers. Second, different TEPs require prospective teachers to attain different levels of content knowledge. We define *content knowledge* as the subject matter taught to a student such as language and science. The level of content knowledge a teacher needs may be indicated by a degree

Figure 4.1. Comparison of Four Teacher Preparation Models

Teacher Education Program	Learning Theory	Content Knowledge	Pedagogical Application	Practicum
Teach for America	Bandura's social cognitive learning theory.	Undergraduate degree combined with independently mastered state requirements.	Pearson and Gallagher's gradual release of responsibility.	3 to 4 weeks.
Montessori	Dr. Montessori's theory on cognitive, motor, and social development based on Piaget and Vygotsky.	Undergraduate degree plus subject teacher training, for example grammar or math.	Montessori Method: student-centered; teacher is a guide to students.	7 weeks.
Finland	Inclusive/ popular learning theories (Piaget, Vygotsky, and Bandura).	Master's degree in major plus half minor.	Content-specific pedagogies (reflection, experimental, creative problem solving).	Approx. 30 weeks.
Singapore	Inclusive/ popular learning theories (Piaget, Vygotsky, and Bandura).	Mastery of content area plus four other major subjects.	Various pedagogies aimed at 21st-century skills (group activities, project-based learning, and inquiry).	20 weeks (additional 10 weeks for graduate work).

requirement or a score on a test. Next, each TEP helps their prospective teachers apply theory to practice by introducing *pedagogical application*, which are the strategies used in the classroom to deliver lessons. Finally, all TEPs require some amount of *practicum experience*, which provides the opportunity for prospective teachers to apply what they learn in a real classroom setting.

Teach for America

History and Key Characteristics. One of the most hotly disputed programs in the United States emerged 25 years ago when Wendy Kopp brought her Princeton senior thesis to life. Kopp recruited 500 graduates from top-performing colleges and universities throughout the country to fill teaching vacancies in some of the country's most underprivileged school districts (Heilig & Jez, 2010). After 2 years in the classroom, she hoped these corps members and prospective teachers would emerge as leaders in education and work to change a national system that frequently limits opportunities for underprivileged children to access a quality education.

Today, Teach for America (TFA) receives heavy criticism for sending seemingly underprepared teachers into high-needs classrooms (Brewer, Kretchmar, Sondel, Ishmael, & Manfra, 2016). Experts such as Thomas Kane produce quantitative evidence for the effectiveness from an economic standpoint, whereas Linda Darling-Hammond has questioned the efficacy of the organization since its early years (Darling-Hammond, 1994; Kane, Rockoff, & Staiger, 2008). However, as Kopp quickly explained during a personal interview, "Teach for America was never meant to be a teacher education program" (Personal communication, March 7, 2016). Today the momentum and the publicity the program has achieved makes it hard to distinguish it from other alternative certification programs. Keeping this in mind, and with its acclaimed success in the classroom, we examine TFA as an alternative teacher education program.

Teach for America's selection process reveals its belief that not everyone can teach. The only prerequisites listed on its website are a bachelor's degree, U.S. citizenship, and a minimum 2.50 undergraduate grade point average (GPA). TFA also lists several characteristics of an effective TFA teacher, including "a deep belief in the potential of all kids and a commitment to do whatever it takes to expand opportunities for students," a "demonstrated leadership ability," and "excellent critical thinking skills," among others (www.teachforamerica.org/join-tfa/is-tfa-for-you).

The process applicants complete to gain admission to the program allows staff members to assess these characteristics. After submitting an online application, selected applicants participate in a phone interview and an online activity. Chosen applicants then participate in a day-long interview experience where they complete an in-person interview, a group activity, and teach a sample practice lesson (Brewer, 2013). Those who effectively display the characteristics TFA looks for are invited into the highly selective community—so selective that in 2010 only 11% of applicants were accepted (Timmerman, 2011).

Learning Theory. Teach for America equips its corps members for success in the classroom through a 4- to 6-week training program called Summer Institute. During this time, corps members teach summer school and attend sessions and workshops that ground them in TFA's main learning theory. Summer Institute itself has changed over the decades, and our most recent research reflects the most prominent trends in TFA since 2010.

In a 2011 publication entitled *Learning Theory*, Teach for America provides a resource to corps members for understanding the most basic and most commonly used models for thinking about thinking and learning (TFA, 2011). In this document, TFA explains why corps members must know learning theory, outlines features of cognitive development at different ages, and provides a framework for understanding different levels of thinking and modes of learning.

The publication identifies Bloom's taxonomy, Howard Gardner's *Theory of Multiple Intelligences*, and emerging research on short-term and long-term memory as the basics of learning theory (TFA, 2011). However, in our research on TFA, we concluded that TFA's learning theory more closely reflects Alfred Bandura's *social cognitive theory*. This theory states that learning is a social endeavor where people learn through observing behaviors and having their own behaviors reinforced (Bandura, 1971). These learning theories lay the groundwork for corps members' work in the classroom.

Content Knowledge. Whereas many American university-sponsored TEPs require candidates to complete a double major or focus to ensure mastery of content knowledge, TFA holds no such requirement—the bachelor's degree application requirement is sufficient. Corps members must ultimately meet state-specific requirements that qualify them as nonconventional teachers, many requirements of which include a test of content knowledge ("Applicant prerequisites," n.d.).

Pedagogical Application. Similar to the coaching required to build any skill, Teach for America provides new teachers with a lesson plan template to help guide corps members' practice of pedagogical application ("Lesson Planning Part I," n.d.). These templates break the lesson down into three large sections: beginning, middle, and end (Farr, 2010). The middle portion of the lesson closely parallels Pearson and Gallagher's (1983) gradual release of responsibility model. Based on this model, teachers begin the lesson by demonstrating the knowledge or the skill (summarized with the buzz phrase "I do it"), then work together with students to develop the skill (referred to as "We do it"), provide space for collaborative learning ("You do it together"), and conclude with the student demonstrating the skill independently ("You do it alone") (Clark, 2014). The goal, by the end of the lesson, is for the student to perform the task or the skill independently. This model depicts the application of Bandura's social cognitive theory both to educating teachers and to teachers educating their students. During Summer Institute, teachers watch practice lessons and practice them under guidance; they then receive their own classroom. They observe, and then their learning is reinforced. Teachers later expect students to master new content using the same model.

Practicum. Teach for America corps members receive little actual classroom experience. During the 5- to 6-week Summer Institute, corps members typically teach one class a day. This class can range from 45 minutes to 2 hours, and the number of students in each class varies dramatically.

> During my own Institute experience, I was lucky if three of my five enrolled students appeared on time, and [I] counted the day an immediate success if there were no dress code violations to address. This was a far cry from the 16 students who greeted me in my own classroom 2 months later.
>
> —Lauren Owen

Once entering their full-time teaching placement in the fall, corps members receive continual professional coaching from a TFA mentor over their 2-year commitment.

Montessori

History and Key Characteristics. In contrast to the quick rise of TFA, the Montessori Method is one of the oldest curricula and pedagogies in use today and has been used for over a century. It has experienced a steady and methodical ascent to its current status, which has attracted followers across the globe. Approximately 22,000 schools are currently affiliated with the program (North American Montessori Teachers' Association, 2016). Dr. Maria Montessori, the first female physician, designed a curriculum, pedagogy, classroom materials, and environment by working with and observing atypically developing children in the Italian slums. This resulted in the *Montessori Method*, a teaching and learning philosophy that encompasses the whole child and her or his development. After great success, where the atypically developing children she taught performed at the same level as typically developing children, she expanded her model to include all children.

Dr. Montessori developed a teacher education program to support her pedagogy. The philosophy of the program is well represented in the quote: "It is not enough for the teacher to love the child. She must first love and understand the universe. She must prepare herself and truly work at it" (Montessori, 1949). For entry, applicants must have earned a bachelor's degree, write an essay, and submit letters of recommendation. Some Montessori programs allow prospective teachers, known as their student-teachers, to simultaneously earn a bachelor's degree and Montessori certification.

Learning Theory. The Montessori Method is both a pedagogy and a learning theory. Montessori developed her own learning theory based on Piaget's (Piaget & Inhelder, 1973) and Vygotsky's (1978) work and through personal observations. She wrote about four distinct planes or stages of child development: Birth to 6, 6 to 12, 12 to 18, and 18 to 24 (Lillard, 2005). The mixed-aged classrooms in a Montessori school are designed around this learning theory, where students progress to the next plane as they exhibit signs of interest and learning in particular materials and lessons. Within each developmental plane, Dr. Montessori's learning theory addresses cognitive, motor, and social development.

Content Knowledge. Unique to the Montessori model of teacher education is its development of content knowledge in student-teachers, which embeds content knowledge in lesson creation. During teacher preparation, student-teachers learn foundational lessons including language, math (geometry and algebra), biology, geography, and music. Student-teachers then practice these content-based lessons by teaching their colleagues—other student-teachers—in a simulated classroom environment. After this, student-teachers instruct students under supervision of qualified teachers during student teaching. Following this practicum period, they are then allowed to instruct their own classroom. Student-teachers also create many of the materials they will later use in their own classroom. This process deepens their understanding of the content and allows their supervisor to evaluate mastery of content knowledge. If a student demonstrates particular interest in a subject, and the content is not available within the classroom, the teacher encourages him or her to go outside of the classroom and into the community for further resources.

Pedagogical Application. The Montessori Method was designed as a holistic, student-centered pedagogy. In the classroom setting, students select their own work and their learning experiences. Parents, teachers, and mentors take cues from the student to guide and direct learning experiences. In order to support the child's innate curiosity and desire to learn and absorb their surroundings, the teacher's role is to spark their imagination through small group lessons and individual interactions. A child will naturally be drawn toward materials that are within their developmental capabilities. Similar to Vygotsky's (1987) *zone of proximal development*, material which is below their developmental level no longer holds their interest, and children will not take much notice of material beyond their developmental level. It is the teacher's responsibility to be a careful observer of her students so that she knows when a child is curious and developmentally ready to be introduced to new materials and lessons. For this reason, the teachers are "guides because they are experts at assisting children to find their own strengths and their own capabilities through the use of practical, self-correcting materials" (AMI/USA, 2014).

Practicum. Before certification, student-teachers spend 4 to 5 weeks of practice teaching with Montessori materials in a classroom without children and instead instruct their peers. Student-teachers then spend approximately 7 weeks in multiple classrooms with a variety of lead teachers. They practice instruction and observe lessons to acquire a well-rounded idea of how teachers run their classrooms. Next, student-teachers enter their own classroom where they are the lead teacher; however, they are still not considered expert teachers until they have had a significant amount of time in the classroom. The back of their teaching certificate is not to be signed until they have acquired 5 years of teaching experience (Tom Postlewaite, personal communication, March 24, 2016).

Finland

History and Key Characteristics. While some TEPs develop independent of governmental backing or guidance, most countries sponsor a variety of teacher education programs. Of these, Finland's stands out. The educational system, which lagged behind its Scandinavian neighbors and was on par with other developing countries such as Malaysia in the 1960s, has become one of the highest-performing internationally (Sahlberg, 2015). Beginning in the 1970s, Finland progressively overhauled its education system by revamping its teacher preparation colleges, increasing the autonomy of teachers, and abolishing school inspection practices.

In Finland, the selectivity of university-based teacher education programs leads to a competitive application process. Finnish universities offer a mere 800 spots every year for prospective primary school teacher (called teacher candidates) and accept only about 1 in 10 applicants (Sahlberg, 2015). While the application is open to anyone eligible for higher education, the multistep process eliminates those who fail to demonstrate high academic performance, strong interpersonal skills, and a deep commitment to students and teaching as a profession. Successful applicants show academic achievement on the VAKAVA exam (a 180-item multiple-choice test based on selected academic articles), a pedagogical exam, an evaluative task, and lastly an in-person interview. This selection process ensures teacher candidates are prepared for the rigors of both the program itself, which requires a master's degree in education (or subjects taught in lower- and upper-secondary schools), and the dynamic needs of students in future classrooms.

Although eight research universities across Finland offer TEPs, the national legislation has standardized the basic content, overall objectives, and minimum credit requirements. Teacher education in Finland is based on a combination of research, practice, and reflection under the autonomy of Finnish universities.

Learning Theory. Finnish TEPs revolve around a research-based preparation approach, which provides candidates with a deep understanding of learning theories. Universities provide a study of a broad base of various learning theories by which candidates understand student growth, including behaviorism, constructivism, and cognitivism. These then become the building blocks for future research projects, as candidates examine the role of learning theory in the classroom. This in-depth knowledge of learning theories equips the teacher to become the researcher, a trademark of the Finnish teacher education system (Jyrhämä et al., 2008).

Content Knowledge. A typical TEP in Finland lasts 5 to 6 years, depending on the field of study a candidate wishes to teach, for example mathematics, science, or music. Candidates supplement learning theories and research methodology with in-depth content learning. A primary school teacher candidate, for example, majors in education and minors in another two subjects taught at primary school (e.g., mathematics and music); a high school teacher candidate majors in the field that they plan to teach and minors in another subject. This model requires the candidate to master the content and the pedagogy for their focus subject.

Pedagogical Application. Finnish teachers apply their pedagogical knowledge and skills in the classroom based on the subject they teach with subject-specific pedagogy. Teacher education in Finland systematically integrates pedagogical content knowledge and practice to enable teachers to enhance their pedagogical thinking and evidence-based decision making in classrooms (Sahlberg, 2015). The combination of these features results in higher levels of autonomy to apply different strategies for pedagogical application depending on the subject.

Practicum. The extent of practical training in Finland's TEPs parallels university teaching hospitals, where universities govern teacher training schools. A teacher candidate completes practical training in teaching schools under a faculty member with an advanced degree in education. Besides the clinical training schools, some teacher candidates also practice in a network of selected municipal public schools. Over a 5-year program, teacher candidates advance from basic teaching to final practice, where they have to deliver independent lessons to different groups of pupils while being evaluated by supervising teachers, education professors, and lecturers. According to Sahlberg (2015), teacher candidates normally spend about 15 to 20% of their study time observing and practicing teaching.

Singapore

History and Key Characteristics. Like Finland, candidates or prospective teachers for Singapore's teacher education program must demonstrate academic mastery. Selected candidates then participate in an interview, where they are evaluated for qualities that Singapore views as implicit for effective teaching: perseverance, interpersonal skills, and commitment. This selection process, along with the positive results of the program, has resulted in teaching being an honored and desired profession (Sclafani, 2015).

Overhauled in 2001, the National Institute of Education (NIE) receives on average 16,000 applications for 2,000 openings in the country's single TEP, which is affiliated with Nanyang Technological University (Sclafani, 2015). The reforms overseen by the Ministry of Education (MOE) emphasize a teacher's career development and pre-service preparation; the MOE hires teachers from the top third of each cohort in the TEP. Teachers then select one of three tracks: the teaching track, the leadership track, or the senior specialist track (Sclafani, 2015). The number of new teachers hired allows administration to anticipate the number of new teachers needed in following years, which helps determine the number of openings in the TEP.

If a candidate is successful in the application process, he or she receives full sponsorship from the government, which includes free tuition, fees and expenses, and a monthly allowance during the TEP. However, if a candidate fails to complete the program successfully, he or she must repay the cost. This becomes a powerful incentive for a candidate to stay in the program. Combined with further support from NIE and the MOE, the attrition rate of teachers leaving the TEP is only about 1% each year (Sclafani, 2015).

Learning Theory. Similar to Finland, Singapore's TEP requires candidates to understand multiple learning theories, ranging from behaviorists to cognitivists, in order to provide a foundation for research. Singapore bases its philosophy of teachers as researchers in the cycle of problem-solving and inquiry learning, where candidates are expected to conduct research in order to learn more about learning (Darling-Hammond & Rothman, 2011). By undertaking research projects during TEP, they examine challenges to teaching and learning, then seek solutions based on the learning theories they are familiar with in order to address student needs in the classroom. In other words, teachers in Singapore use new strategies to address the diverse problems that they may face in their own classroom.

Content Knowledge. Teacher candidates in Singapore are given flexibility to choose an arts- or science-based subject to pursue during the TEP. This equips them with the content knowledge that is relevant for the classroom when they graduate. For primary-level teacher programs, candidates are trained in one content area and are also prepared in the four mandatory subjects (English, mathematics, science, and social studies) that they must teach (Darling-Hammond & Rothman, 2011). At the secondary level, teacher candidates must master two academic subjects that they will teach based on their chosen track, for example arts, science, or combination. In general, TEPs in Singapore require teachers to acquire mastery of fundamental subjects and chosen specialties.

Pedagogical Application. During their preparation, teacher candidates take specific courses to learn to apply theory to classroom practice. Central among the strategies they use are instructional design and technology and effective classroom management. As part of the product of a system-wide reform called "Thinking Schools, Learning Nation," a vision for a total learning environment that "describes a nation of thinking and committed citizens capable of meeting future challenges and an education system geared to the needs of the 21st century," teacher candidates learn to develop students' 21st-century skills through the group activities and project-based learning that they experienced in their own TEP (Deng, 2004). Project-based learning is a pedagogical approach where students develop required content knowledge and skills by working for an extended period of time on a project. These projects are designed to support students in investigating real-world challenges. Candidates then also adapt pedagogy as it relates to the culture, history, and philosophical view of educational issues and problems.

Practicum. From early on in their training, teacher candidates are exposed to classrooms through practicum work. Candidates observe, assist, and learn with NIE professors who work closely with teachers and administrators in schools. These professors report on candidates' performance. Practical training is done through an enhanced school partnership model, which is characterized by a three-way relationship between NIE, MOE, and schools that wish to participate in teacher education programs (NIE, 2010). Candidates spend more than 20 weeks during a 4-year undergraduate program working in partner schools, while a 10-week practicum is expected for a 1-year graduate program (NIE, 2010). To support the process of teaching, TEPs expose teacher candidates to model classrooms that are introducing new teaching strategies.

THE LENS TEACHING THEORIES PROVIDE

The debate around who can teach often centers on teacher education programs (TEPs). We've seen how a variety of TEPs seek to prepare teachers through similar program components. However, to understand the complexity of teacher growth over their career, considering TEPs through the lens of teaching theory provides an understanding of the long-term development of teachers beyond the traditional responsibilities of TEPs.

Teaching, like learning, is a developmental process, and critical experiences after completion of a TEP lead to teachers becoming effective lifelong learners, which allows them continuously to add to their knowledge and skills (Darling-Hammond & Bransford, 2005, p. 3). Therefore, TEPs are only one component of answering the question, "Can anyone teach?" To fully respond to this question, we need a clearer understanding of the developmental process a teacher undergoes and how TEPs factor into this process.

Teaching theory encompasses the individual evolution of a teacher as he or she grows through continuous self-evaluation, interactions, experiences, and deliberate practice (Rodriguez & Solis, 2013). Viewing TEPs through the lens of teaching theory equips teachers, school systems, policymakers, and TEPs to design education and professional development that support teacher growth. One way this growth can be measured is along a spectrum, such as that presented in Figure 4.2. As a teacher grows, descriptors can be used as a signal to indicate where a teacher falls on the spectrum. In contrast to characteristics, descriptors

Figure 4.2. Descriptors on a Spectrum of Teacher Development

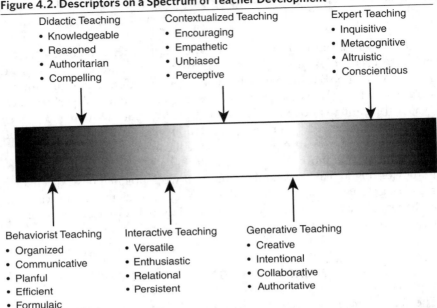

are adjectives that describe the teacher at a point along the spectrum. Teaching theory provides a lens through which teachers can reflect on their movement along the spectrum.

This spectrum becomes a tool for schools, TEPs, and teachers. With this spectrum, schools can effectively differentiate professional development to lead to teacher growth. TEPs can then evaluate where a teacher is at upon entry and exit into the program and then guide the candidate to an environment that will continue his or her professional development. Teachers can use the spectrum to identify their position on the spectrum and use teaching theory to strategize their goals and growth.

Education research from Linda Darling-Hammond and John Bransford (2005) describe a teacher's growth as a developmental trajectory. This trajectory merges concept with practice and guides the teacher in reflection on their skill set. However, Darling-Hammond and Bransford also recognize the challenge of defining this developmental trajectory:

> Figuring out how specific learning opportunities and teacher education practices can capitalize on [teacher development]—and what the results are—is

in some ways the most complex kind of research, because it requires tracking not only what and how teachers learn, but also how they use what they have learned and to what effect. (p. 29)

Similar to the way in which teachers apply their content knowledge and learning theory through pedagogical application, educators need tools to apply teacher development and teaching theory to TEPs. As a result, TEPs will be better positioned to move teachers to the desired point upon the spectrum. The question shifts from "Can anyone teach?" to "How do teachers develop?"

CONCLUSION

Answering the question "Can anyone teach?" with a simple yes or no ultimately negates the complexity of teacher development and begs further questions, such as:

1. What skills can a TEP begin to seed in teachers so that they can continue growth after entering the classroom?
2. What strategies or processes help teachers grow across the spectrum of teaching?
3. What can we look for as evidence of a developmental teaching theory?
4. How does the spectrum support teachers finding their place along their developmental path?

Based solely on our research into teacher education programs (TEPs), we realized we cannot speculate which individuals can or should teach, particularly within the real-world scenario of teaching in a classroom. TEPs reveal only one part of teacher development.

What we can conclude is that TEPs play an important role in helping a teacher understand his or her development. TEPs currently utilize their own combinations and beliefs to produce what they believe are teachers equipped for the classroom. However, teacher growth does not stop once the TEP is completed. By placing the growth a teacher achieves during a TEP in the context of a developmental teaching theory, teachers can better understand their own strengths and focus on areas of long-term growth. We, therefore, suggest further research in a developmental teaching theory to advance conversation around teacher development.

REFERENCES

AMI/USA. (2014). *The Montessori teacher*. Retrieved from http://amiusa.org/
Applicant prerequisites. (n.d.). Retrieved from https://www.teachforamerica.org/
teach-with-tfa/tfa-and-you/applicant-prerequisites
Bandura, A. (1971). *Social learning theory*. New York, NY: General Learning Press.
Brewer, T. J. (2013). From the trenches: A Teach for America corps member's perspective. *Critical Education, 4*(12), 1–17. Retrieved from http://ojs.library.ubc
.ca/index.php/criticaled/article/view/183939
Brewer, T. J., Kretchmar, K., Sondel, B., Ishmael, S., & Manfra, M. M. (2016). Teach
for America's preferential treatment: School district contracts, hiring decisions,
and employment practices. *Education Policy Analysis Archives, 24*(15), 1–31.
Clark, S. (2014). Avoiding the blank stare: Teacher training with the gradual release
of responsibility in mind. *English Teaching Forum, 28–35*.
Darling-Hammond, L. (1994). Who will speak for the children? How "Teach for
America" hurts urban schools and students. *Phi Delta Kappan, 76*(1), 21–34.
Retrieved from http://www.jstor.org/stable/20405253.
Darling-Hammond, L., & Bransford, J. (Eds.). (2005). *Preparing teachers for a
changing world: What teachers should learn and be able to do*. San Francisco,
CA: Jossey-Bass A Wiley Imprint.
Darling-Hammond, L., & Rothman, R. (Eds.). (2011). Teacher and leader effectiveness in high-performing education systems, *Alliance for Excellent Education*.
Deng, Z. (2004). Beyond teacher training: Singaporean teacher preparation in the
era of new educational initiatives. *Teaching Education, 15*(2), 159–173.
Farr, S. (2010). *Teaching as leadership*. San Francisco, CA: Jossey-Bass.
Heilig, J. V., & Jez, S. J. (2010). Teach for America: A review of the evidence. *Boulder
and Tempe: Education and the Public Interest Center & Education Policy Research Unit*. Retrieved from http://epicpolicy.org/publication/teach-for-america
Jyrhämä, R., Kynäslahti, H., Krokfors, L., Byman, R., Maaranen, K., Toom, A., &
Kansanen, P. (2008). The appreciation and realisation of research-based teacher
education: Finnish students' experiences of teacher education. *European Journal of Teacher Education, 31*(1), 1–16.
Kane, T. J., Rockoff, J. E., & Staiger, D. O. (2008). What does certification tell us
about teacher effectiveness? Evidence from New York City. *Economics of Education Review, 27*(6), 615–631. doi: 10.1016/j.econedurev.2007.05.005
Lesson Planning Part I. (n.d.). Retrieved from http://teachingasleadership.org/sites/
default/files/Related-Readings/IPD_Ch5_2011.pdf
Lillard, A. S. (2005). *Montessori: The science behind the genius*. New York, NY: Oxford
University Press, Inc.
Montessori, M. (1949). *The absorbent mind*. Madras, India: Kalakshetra.
National Institute of Education (NIE). (2010). A teacher education model for the
21st century: TE 21 [PowerPoint presentation]. Singapore: Author.
North American Montessori Teachers' Association. (2016). *How many Montessori schools are there?* Retrieved from http://www.montessori-namta.org/FAQ/
Montessori-Education/How-many-Montessori-schools-are-there
Piaget, J. & Inhelder, B. (1973). *Memory and intelligence*. London, England: Routledge & Kegan Paul.

Pearson, P. D., & Gallagher, M. (1983). The instruction of reading comprehension. *Contemporary Educational Psychology*, 8, 317–344.

Rodriguez, V., & Fitzpatrick, M. (2014). *The teaching brain: An evolutionary trait at the heart of education*. New York: The New Press.

Rodriguez, V., & Solis, S. L. (2013). Teachers' awareness of the learner-teacher interaction: Preliminary communication of a study investigating the teaching brain. *Mind, Brain, and Education, 7*(3), 161–169. doi:10.1111/mbe.12023

Sahlberg, P. (2015). *Finnish lessons 2.0: What can the world learn from educational change in Finland*. New York, NY: Teachers College Press.

Sclafani, S. (2015). *Singapore chooses teachers carefully*. 97(3), 8–13.

Teach for America (TFA) (2011). *Learning Theory*. Retrieved from http://teachingas-leadership.org/sites/default/files/Related-Readings/LT_2011.pdf

Timmerman, M. B. (2011). TFA: A corporate approach. *Harvard Crimson*. Retrieved from http://www.thecrimson.com/article/2011/9/29/tfa-harvard-students-education/

United Nations. (2015). *The Millennium Development Goals report*. New York, NY: Author.

Vygotsky, L. S. (1978). *Mind and society: The development of higher psychological processes*. Cambridge, MA: Harvard University Press.

Vygotsky, L. S. (1987). *The collected works of L. S. Vygotsky*. New York, NY: Plenum Press.

CHAPTER 5

Do We Still Need Teacher Unions?

Aditi Adhikari, Jason Brown, and Amanda Klonsky

In this chapter we explore the question: Do we still need teacher unions? Through perspectives from Kathmandu to Chicago, we investigate the role of teacher unions internationally. In fact, this chapter is written in response to the following questions posed by fellow students at the Harvard Graduate School of Education: Are teacher unions still necessary? Do they play a progressive or a regressive role in current school reform efforts? We are graduate students in education, with different lived experiences with regard to teacher unions. Aditi grew up in Nepal during the civil war and had a negative view of teacher unions, colored by her experiences with corruption and violence during the conflict. Amanda grew up in a family of teachers and labor organizers in the heart of post-industrial Chicago and worked in Chicago public schools as a social worker. Jason was raised in Arizona, a right-to-work state where there are no teacher unions; he now enjoys the benefits of union membership as a teacher in Washington, DC.

AN OVERVIEW OF TEACHER UNIONS

These case studies from Nepal, the United States, and Northern Europe present unions in various states of conflict or collaboration with government. In each case, unions have helped to improve educational and economic conditions for both children and teachers and have contributed to economic development and democratic governance in society at large.

In Chicago, we see a relationship of both conflict and collaboration in the context of a major American city, where public sector unions are under attack. In Northern Europe, we explore what is possible when government and unions work together toward systemic improvement. In Nepal, we explore the role of teacher unions in the context of a post-war, developing country. In each example, we see that teacher unions can be a force not only for better working conditions for teachers but for improved learning conditions for students, as well as toward social justice, equality, and strengthened democracy.

United States

Today, only about 1 in 10 workers in the United States are unionized. Despite evidence that strong unions help create a strong middle class, reduce economic inequality, and increase economic viability in cities, this anti-union trend is moving into states that were once union strongholds.

> From record-high union membership in the 1940s and 1950s when a third of the workforce was unionized, the United States now only boasts a meager 11.1% of unionized employees. Further, lowering membership numbers in the United States are negatively correlated with a greater disparity in wealth. As this trend continues, we may see even greater economic despair on our country's hardest-working employees. (Mishel & Schieder, 2016)

Teachers remain one of the most heavily unionized sectors of American labor, but even teacher unions have seen a decline due to many factors, including the rise of nonunion charter schools, which in some cities teach up to a third of the student population. Teacher unions face attacks as do all other public sector unions from those who claim that public sector employee unions waste taxpayer dollars and protect bad employees. The National Education Association (NEA) is the largest labor union in the United States, with just under 3 million members (NEA, n.d.). The American Federation of Teachers (AFT) has 1.6 million members in more than 3,000 local affiliates nationwide (AFT, n.d.). Public schools have seen a decline in student population overall, especially in urban districts, due to the expansion of privately run charter schools. In Chicago, charter schoolteachers are not allowed to be members of the same local unions as their 20,000-plus colleagues in the Chicago Teachers Union (CTU). A new union, the Association of Charter School Teachers (ACTS), was formed in recent years and has succeeded in organizing teacher unions in a few charter schools (Vevea, 2011), but charter sector unionization is extremely difficult, and conflict exists as to whether charters are truly public schools and subject to the same laws under the National Labor Relations Board (NLRB), which protects the right to organize.

A look at the education systems in the United States provides evidence that teacher unions support economic development and strengthen systems of public education to better serve students as well as teachers. The states that have outlawed union membership, known as *right-to-work* states, such as Arizona, Florida, and Mississippi, often have the highest rates of poverty, the poorest school districts, and the worst educational outcomes for students (Education Week Research Center, 2016). Mississippi schools score the lowest on the NAEP and receive the second-lowest funding per pupil in the nation. The U.S. child poverty rate ranks second-worst among the world's developed countries, and Mississippi has the highest child poverty rate in the United States. Over 35% of Mississippi's children fall under the international poverty standard as defined by the United Nations Children's Fund (UNICEF, 2012). In contrast to Mississippi, Massachusetts has always had a strong teacher union and is also ranked among the top public education systems in the nation. Of course, these inequalities have deep roots in the South, beginning with the system of slavery, and cannot be attributed to unionization alone, but it is clear that teacher unions reduce educational inequality and improve learning conditions for students as well as working conditions for teachers overall.

The first teacher union in the United States, the Chicago Teachers Federation, was formed in 1897 by Margaret Haley and Catherine Goggin. Dana Goldstein's history of the period tells us that Haley's views were akin to those of today's leaders of the CTU (Goldstein, 2012). Some prominent turn-of-the-century education reformers in the United States thought the problem with urban schools was that women weren't sufficiently intellectual, as they were not college educated, and were, therefore, ineffective teachers. Instead of expanding access to college education for women, these critics called for increased standardization in the profession. Haley saw female educators not as the problem but as part of the solution. She wanted to try a different way of running schools, one that increased budgets but relied less on centralization and more on the instincts of individual educators with ties to the communities in which they worked.

More than 100 years later, these hard questions and debates persist. Do we improve public education through increased standardization—the Common Core, high-stakes testing, scripted curriculum—or do we attempt to give educators and parents the power to determine what is best for their students? Do we improve teacher quality by scripting their lessons for them, or do we try to raise the level of the profession in society by advancing teacher education and pay along with the standards of entrance into the profession?

In June of 2011, former Illinois Governor Patrick Quinn signed into law Senate Bill 7 (SB7) prohibiting teacher unions from calling a strike with less than 75% of member approval. This requirement for an unprecedented level of approval was presumed by lawmakers to be unattainable. Thus, they assumed that they had crippled the CTU by making teacher strikes impossible, if not illegal, in Illinois.

The private lobby group Stand for Children bankrolled the lobbying for SB7. The organization's director, Jonah Edelman, was caught on video at the Aspen Institute bragging about his efforts to undermine the union's ability to strike (McQueary, 2011). The video went viral during contract negotiations. CTU took the issue to their members and received the overwhelming approval needed to approve a strike. Teacher leaders in 150 schools polled union members, and well over 75% of teachers at each school favored a strike if contract negotiations failed.

Under SB7, CTU is legally bound to represent the members—Chicago's 26,000 teachers—on wage and benefit issues only. They are forbidden by law from negotiating on issues such as class size, working conditions, and other justice issues. In spite of this, the union ultimately went on strike, with these nonsalary issues at the forefront.

The Chicago Teachers Union had been in negotiations with the Chicago Board of Education since November 2011, and over a year of talks had already taken place without much progress. The CTU struck on September 10, 2012, and 26,000 members picketed in front of their local school buildings and then marched on the CPS Central Office in one of the largest labor demonstrations in Chicago in decades. Despite SB7, the main issues on the table were benefits, job security, teacher evaluations, and class size. Remarkably, the press reported strong public support for the strike, especially among Chicago public school parents, despite the inconvenience and the disruption of having the schools closed. This public support inarguably strengthened the hand of the union in contract negotiations (Associated Press, 2012).

After nearly 2 weeks on the picket line on the broiling hot Chicago streets, negotiations finally yielded an agreement. The union negotiating team brought the proposed contract to their delegates, who in turn shared the proposal with the members. The union leadership resisted pressure from the mayor to settle the strike in closed-door meetings with him. Instead, all over the city, on the final day of the strike, teachers sat in clusters of folding chairs in front of their locked school buildings, reading and discussing the hundreds of pages of the contract. The process was an extraordinary example of democracy—every teacher engaging in the decision as to whether the union's house of delegates should approve this contract and end the strike.

In the end, the strike forced CPS to restore a cap on class size, eliminating their previous plan to increase class size to as many as 45 students per classroom. The plan to evaluate teachers based on students' standardized test scores alone was rolled back. CPS committed to installing air conditioning in every dangerously hot classroom. A compromise was reached. The union voted to end the strike on September 18, 2012, and students returned to school the next day.

Since that time, the CTU has faced big challenges. In 2013, the school board closed 49 neighborhood schools, nearly all in low-income, black and brown neighborhoods. Illinois Governor Bruce Rauner, a Republican, refused to sign a state budget, demanding a rollback in union rights in exchange for state funding. As a result of this crisis, Chicago teachers faced new rounds of layoffs, and in the late summer of 2016, the school board fired 1,000 CPS employees, including more than 500 teachers and 500 classroom aides and other staff.

Although the CTU faces battles that are central to its very existence, the union continues to organize beyond the bread-and-butter issues of salaries and job protections. The union is active in the broader movements for social justice in Chicago, supporting protests against police violence and against cuts of public health, mental health, and employment programs. CTU has taken a stand against the increasing police presence in schools and called for an end to the police killings of black youth in Chicago. The union has become a force in progressive electoral politics in Chicago. CTU has endorsed and organized for political candidates for Chicago mayor and for pro-labor candidates for other elected offices.

The Chicago Teachers Union has become an engine for social equality not only in the public schools but in the city at large. In this sense, CTU can serve as a model for the rebirth of the American labor movement, showing what is possible when unions move beyond fighting on economic issues only and join together with larger movements for justice.

Northern Europe

The education systems in Nordic countries are typically regarded as high quality, inclusive, and equitable. This is partly due to the ideals of a strong welfare state, where taxes and government subsidies fund public goods available to all regardless of ethnicity, socioeconomic standing, or minority status. The profession of teaching is widely respected in these societies and even requires a master's degree education with a mandatory research component in both Norway and Finland. Many of the advances in the professionalization of teaching can be attributed to the strong networks of teacher unions in these countries.

The number of teacher–student contact hours in all Nordic countries falls below the OECD average, while teacher salaries hover around the OECD average, feats that are often associated with powerful teacher unions (OECD, 2015). In contrast to unions' roles in the United States, it is not just the bread-and-butter issues that provide the strength and the importance of labor unions in Nordic educational spheres. Despite what critics say about these socialist nanny states, the Scandinavian countries boast an education system anchored in equity and quality. Teacher unions in Norway and Finland are pushing to elevate the teaching profession and advance equity among its citizens. These engaged unions, working in close collaboration with their respective governments, have given the profession a strong voice at the table and a leading role in social change.

Approximately 90% of the teachers in Norway belong to the Union of Education Norway, the nation's largest teacher union (B. E. Aaslid, personal communication, March 15, 2016). They encourage school administrators to join as well, as they stress the need for all school employees to stand unified. There is even an autonomous branch specifically for students in teacher education programs, with a place on the union's executive board to voice the student perspective. The foremost role of the Union of Education Norway and its student branch is to work in close collaboration with the government to advance the teaching profession and ensure quality instruction for all of Norway's students.

Norway has been in the process of revamping its entire teacher education program, with full union support. After grieving from PISA shock and mediocre teacher quality, the country is ready to take on initial teacher education and better prepare its aspiring educators. The shift from a 4-year, largely theoretical degree to a 5-year, research-based education is a big adjustment, but nearly everyone favors this boost in rigor. Where union and government differ is in the coursework that con- stitutes the degree. The Ministry of Education is adamantly pushing for a larger portion of the lengthened degree to be spent in content-specific didactics classes. The union, however, is pushing for a more balanced curriculum with a focus on both content and general pedagogy.

While a disagreement in policy is common between a trade union and the government, where this relationship surpasses the norm is the amount of conversation between the two parties. When there are open discussions between a union and its governmental counterpart, there is opportunity to find compromise and a solution that satisfies both par- ties. A Norwegian union official writes, "There is consensus that educa- tion is of utmost importance for the nation and that teachers are the most important factor for student learning. Therefore, educational issues are easily set on the agenda" (Bascia & Osmond, 2013).

Finland also places strong emphasis on union-government collaboration. In fact, Finland may have one of the tightest such partnerships, which could help explain the country's rise to educational stardom with a highly respected teaching force.

Finland boasts a teacher union with membership that exceeds 95%, representing teachers from early childhood to the university level (Trade Union of Education in Finland—OAJ, n.d.). The main teacher union, the Trade Union of Education, is a member of the larger confederation of academic professionals known as Akava. This umbrella organization includes affiliates from other respected professions, including the Finnish Medical Association, Union of Professional Engineers, and the Association of Finnish Lawyers. It is no wonder that nearly all Finnish teachers voluntarily join this nonpolitical professional body. When teachers are represented by the same union organization as other revered professionals, it adds prestige to the once more modest career.

The teacher union, with assistance from Akava, is involved in a tripartite relationship with the government and school systems. None of these sectors can push policy or enact reform without consensus among all stakeholders. One major feat accomplished by Finland's teacher union and the Ministry of Education and Culture is the complete overhaul of the teaching profession. As in Norway, Finnish teachers are well respected and receive trust and autonomy from the government. Class sizes have been reduced over the years, and becoming a teacher has become more selective. These reforms in the past several decades were enacted with the teacher union's full support and presence at the bargaining table.

Of course, the strong teacher union is not the sole reason for recent Finnish educational success. However, many of Finland's exemplary features are closely linked with the union's efforts to elevate the profession and create close collaboration with the government. While in many parts of the world there is political conflict between these typically warring factions, Finland's previous Minister of Education explained, "Our teachers' union has been one of the main partners because we have the same goal. . . . They are very good partners for us" (Snider, 2011).

The Norwegian and Finnish national teacher unions, or teacher association as they should be called, are a good example of functional collaboration between unions and government. The governments of Norway and Finland see the teacher unions as partners in a mutual effort to strengthen the systems of public education. Disagreement and conflict still occur, but this working relationship allows for significant negotiation on policy and improvements to the teaching profession and strengthens social equality in education and beyond.

Nepal

Educational inequality in Nepal has deep historical roots. Before 1951, Nepal was ruled by the Rana oligarchy, which considered education a threat to their power. Since then, Nepal has gone through two political revolutions, in 1990 and 2006, and is now established as the Federal Democratic Republic of Nepal. Between 1996 and 2006, a civil war caused extensive damage to educational infrastructure. Scores of teachers were killed by both the Maoists and security forces during this time.

Since the war, Nepal has made big strides in education. Nepal's literacy rate increased from 55.5% in the 1995–1996 fiscal year to 84.7% in the 2011–2012 fiscal year (UNESCO, 2015). In spite of these steps forward, inequalities in access to the education system remain vast; disparities in school enrollment and attainment are based on gender, caste hierarchy, and social class. As a consequence, in 2014, 90.2% of students from private schools but only 39.8% of students from public schools passed the school-leaving certificate at the end of 10th grade (Government of Nepal, 2015). Privatization of public education is increasing; enrollment in private schools was less than 7% in 2005 and had reached 16% by 2013. According to data from 2011 (Bhatta, 2014), most private schools are registered as companies, allowing them to make a profit.

Nepal's teacher union movement started in 1980 with the *Nepal Rastriya Sikshak Sangathan* (Nepal National Teachers Association, NNTA), which sought to provide teachers with benefits comparable to those of other government employees. According to Badri Prasad Khatiwada, founding chairperson of the NNTA, the association was not affiliated with any political party (Biswakarma, 2008). In fact, the teacher union became a legal constitutional entity when political parties were still banned by the active monarchy.

The NNTA participated in the democratic movement of 1990 because the teachers in the union decided that their rights were always going to be compromised unless there was democracy in the country (Tilak Kunwar, personal communication, August 11, 2016). Multiparty democracy was reinstated in April 1990. Accusations that the NNTA was affiliated to the Communist Party of Nepal (Unified Marxist-Leninist) led many of its members to quit. In June 1990, the Nepali congress called a meeting of all teachers who supported their party. The Nepal Teachers Association was thus formed. In the following years, other teacher unions were formed in affiliation with the other major political parties.

Political parties encouraged the politicization of teachers by giving them an office within their party offices. Given the government's indifference towards teachers, the sense of security provided by political parties was reassuring. The teacher union movement thus became divided along party lines, and these divisions have limited their work as independent professional unions.

The Seventh Amendment of Nepal's Education Act (1970) passed in 2001, which guaranteed the right of each teacher to be affiliated with one teacher union, to protect their rights and welfare (Bista, 2006). Shortly thereafter, there was an effort by the various teacher unions to create a unified teacher union movement. Although teacher unions managed to work across party lines, the movement remained divided by political ideologies. Three umbrella organizations emerged.

By 2014, even the Communist Party of Nepal (Maoist), which had entered mainstream politics after the peace agreements in 2006, had led two coalition governments. Teachers in the union movement felt that no matter which political party was in power, little was done to elevate the status of teachers. In 2014, discussions between teachers in all three umbrella associations led them to conclude that it was not worthwhile to be divided based on political ideology, and they started organizing together. In September 2014, teachers launched a protest demanding that the more than 50,000 teachers hired on temporary contracts across Nepal receive pay, benefits, and retirement packages equal to permanent teachers ("Temp teachers want equal pay," 2014). As a part of the protests, they padlocked the account offices in the Department of Education, as well as the District Education offices in all 75 districts. As a result of this protest, in July 2015, the Ministry of Education and Teachers' Service Commission offered temporary teachers a golden handshake: a limited retirement payout for teachers who would have otherwise had no retirement benefits and the promise of priority in hiring processes for permanent teachers. These victories for the improved status of teachers would not have been possible without teacher unions.

In February 2015, the three teacher union coalitions were dissolved, and the Confederation of Nepalese Teachers (CNT), an umbrella organization of 16 teacher unions, was founded with the motto "teacher's unity for rights and responsibilities" (Confederation of Nepali Teachers, 2015) As a united movement, the CNT will continue struggling for their rights and attempt to collaborate with the government for educational change. "From 1980 to 2014, we focused on trade union rights and not our responsibilities as teachers," says Tilak Kunwar, secretary general of the CNT (personal communication, August 11, 2016). "If we raise our voice for students' futures and educational change, students and parents will support our fight for our rights, too."

Currently, the CNT is fighting for teachers to have an active role in planning the new educational reform initiatives, with the firm belief that no program will be effective unless teachers are informed, ready, and motivated. The CNT has organized a national conference and two regional conferences about the School Sector Development Plan, the government's new education plan for 2016 through 2023. In addition, the CNT sent teacher leaders from all 75 districts to spread awareness about the targets within the UN's Sustainable Development Goal 4, "Quality Education," which will inform the government's plans in education.

The CNT's code of conduct dictates that individual teachers put education and the needs of teachers before the individual teacher organizations to which they belong, but the CNT is an umbrella organization of teacher unions, most of which are still affiliated to political parties, and teachers cannot join as individual members. When asked whether the CNT can one day be completely free of the politically affiliated organizations that comprise it, Kunwar says, "There might be a day when we decide that we have the same purpose, and we might refuse to fly the flags of different political parties. In that case, we could decide to dissolve the unions, and the CNT could become an organization of members" (personal communication, August 11, 2016).

Local elections have not occurred in Nepal since 1997. An entire generation of local leaders has not been able to contest elections, and schools are one of the few public institutions where they can engage in politics. As Nepal progresses into a more stable democracy where local elections are held regularly, it is possible that Nepal's teacher unions will continue to strengthen their ties to one another to unite around educational equity and improving working conditions for teachers in Nepal. This would be a step toward a strengthened system of public education in Nepal.

CONCLUSION

Despite the vastly different contexts and conditions of teachers as workers in the United States, the Nordic countries and Nepal it is clear that teacher unions are still needed, both to defend the rights of teachers as employees and to work for the improvement of educational systems. Effective teacher unions or professional associations must evolve with the changing needs of their education systems, and unions should look to one another globally for models of improvement. To be sure, teacher unions around the world must change (Tucker, 2012). Alberta Teachers Association in Canada, Swedish Teachers' Union, and Australian Education Union are examples of modern, professional organizations that perceive educational development as a whole, not just protection of the teaching profession as their central mission. High-performing school systems, including those that perform well on the PISA, have strong, institutionalized teacher unions that operate independently and are embraced by the government as important actors and even as collaborating partners. Systems that seek to improve their education systems would be well advised to strengthen their unions rather than demeaning, restricting, or even abolishing them.

REFERENCES

American Federation of Teachers (AFT). (n.d.). *About us.* Retrieved from http://www.aft.org/about#sthash.0GMKZOge.dpuf

Associated Press. (2012). Parents support Chicago teachers but for how long? *Fox News Politics.* September 11. Retrieved from http://www.foxnews.com/politics/2012/09/11/chicago-parents-scramble-to-find-safe-place-for-students-as-teacher-strike.html

Bascia, N., & Osmond, P. (2013). *Teacher union–governmental relations in the context of educational reform,* p. 14. Retrieved from http://download.ei-ie.org/Docs/WebDepot/Teacher_Union_Study.pdf

Bhatta, S. D. (2014). Nepal private sector engagement in school education [PowerPoint presentation]. Retrieved from https://olc.worldbank.org/sites/default/files/Session%203.pdf

Bista, M. B. (2006). *Status of female teachers in Nepal.* Kathmandu, Nepal: United Nations Educational, Scientific and Cultural Organization.

Biswakarma, B. (2008). *Sikshak Rajniti: Daliya Rajniti bata Mukta Hunai Parchha* [Teacher politics: must be free from party politics]. *Sikshak Masik,* 03, 12–13.

UNESCO. (2015). Education for All: National Review Report, 2001–2015. Retrieved from http://unesdoc.unesco.org/images/0023/002327/232769E.pdf

Confederation of Nepali Teachers. (2015). *Code of conduct.*

Education Week Research Center. (2016, January 7). Measuring up: Latest scorecard puts states, nation to the test. *Education Week.* Retrieved from http://www.edweek.org/ew/articles/2016/01/07/2016-education-rankings-put-states-nation-to-the-test.html

Goldstein, D. (2012). *The Chicago strike and the history of American teachers' unions* September 12. Retrieved from http://www.danagoldstein.com/2012/09/the-chicago-strike-and-the-history-of-american-teachers-unions.html

Government of Nepal. (2015). *Nepal education in figures 2015 at-a-glance.* Kathmandu: Ministry of Education.

McQueary, K. (2011). Education group tries to rebound after diatribe. *New York Times.* December 2. Retrieved from http://www.nytimes.com/2011/12/02/us/education-group-tries-to-rebound-after-diatribe.html

Mishel, L., & Schieder, J. (2016). As union membership has fallen, the top 10 percent have been getting a larger share of income. *Economic Policy Institute.* May 24.

Retrieved from http://www.epi.org/publication/as-union-membership-has-fallen-the-top-10-percent-have-been-getting-a-larger-share-of-income

National Education Association (NEA). (n.d.). *About*. Retrieved from http://www.nea.org/home/2580.htm

OECD. (2015). *Education at a glance 2015: OECD indicators*. OECD Publishing. Retrieved from http://dx.doi.org/10.1787/eag-2015-en

Snider, J. (2011, March 16). *The Hechinger report: An interview with Henna Virkkunen, Finland's minister of education*. Retrieved from http://hechingerreport.org/an-interview-with-henna-virkkunen-finlands-minister-of-education/

Temp teachers want equal pay. (2014). *Kathmandu Post*. Retrieved from http://kathmandupost.ekantipur.com/news/2014-09-24/temp-teachers-want-equal-pay.html

Trade Union of Education in Finland—OAJ. (n.d.). Retrieved from http://www.oaj.fi/cs/oaj/trade%20union%20of%20education%20in%20finland

Tucker, M. (2012). A different role for teachers' unions. *Education Next, 12*(1). Retrieved from http://educationnext.org/a-different-role-for-teachers-unions/

UNICEF. (2012). *Measuring child poverty: New league tables of child poverty in the world's richest countries*. Florence, Italy: UNICEF Office of Research Innocenti.

Vevea, R. (2011). Unions move in at Chicago charter schools, and resistance is swift. *American Federation of Teachers*. Retrieved from http://www.aftacts.org/charter-news/152-unions-move-in-at-chicago-charter-schools-and-resistance-is-swift

CHAPTER 6

Will Technology Make Schools Smarter?

Chu Chen, Reema Souraya, and Kolja Wohlleben

"Am I late again?" you wonder, calling up your watch. Blue letters light up on your right contact lens: 8:45 a.m., plenty of time before the first lesson. You decided to walk to school today as spring has set in, and a little morning exercise usually helps you focus during the day. Music in your ear, you don't hear your friend Jaime calling you from the other side of the street, so he runs over to greet you. You walk the rest of the way together, discussing math homework and sharing a sandwich. Math is your strongest subject. The ClassWhizz system notified your dad yesterday: It would transfer 15 EduCoins to you, and it encouraged him to buy you the shoes you so desperately want and had searched for online. To Jamie, math doesn't come as naturally. Not only did he not earn any EduCoins, he also stopped practicing early. ClassWhizz notified his parents right away. Despite multiple admonitions by the system, after just 10 minutes of practicing fractions, Jamie had put the ClassWhizz goggles away and started reading his book. His parents were not pleased. If he continued to work so sloppily, they said, his records would not allow him to study engineering. As of now, Jaime's skill points are only in the 7th percentile. Over the remaining 7 years of school, he can't afford to read as many novels, or he'll risk scoring low on the behavioral scales.

You have made your way to school and are now entering the classroom. You give a quick nod to Mr. Khan, who is checking the latest ClassWhizz report. He doesn't seem happy; the bell rings, and he tells you why. Apparently several of your classmates have emulated Jaime. They tossed their goggles away in order to draw, paint, read, listen to music, or play ball outside. Mr. Khan is a veteran teacher who has not always worked with ClassWhizz, and you can tell. It's not that he can't handle the technology, but he seems less than earnest when scolding students based on the Whizz's report. While you adjust the goggles, you wonder what school looked like when he started working 35 years ago. The screen lights up, and the familiar deep female voice addresses you:

> Good morning! It is 9:05 a.m., April 23, 2051. From the crumbs on your shirt, I see you have just finished your breakfast. According to your usual neuronal activity at this time of the day, I propose some new calculus content for the next 20 minutes. Your normal blood pressure curve during light exercise has proven to be helpful for your long-term memory performance. Why don't we go on a walk afterwards so you can learn some Chinese vocabulary? If you agree with this training plan, please say "Okay learning." If you want to propose changes, say "Change plan," and I will see what we can adjust. Please answer in the next minute, or a human assistant will facilitate the process.

BRAVE NEW WORLD OF EDUCATION

Writers and filmmakers of utopian or dystopian worlds are not as detached from the real world as many think. In fact, their work is usually an attempt at extrapolating what is happening currently and to paint possible futures. We believe that the world of you, Jaime, Mr. Khan, and ClassWhizz is one such possible future. This chapter is an attempt to coherently explore the question of whether technology will eventually unleash intended change in education, as many of its advocates promise, and what trends the future might bring with it. This is indeed one of the hard questions in global education. With the diversity in technologies and beliefs, some other important questions continue to emerge. For instance: Do digital devices change our intellectual behaviors and brain physiology, and if so, how and what does it mean for teachers and learning in schools? Can machines teach us some things better than humans? Is there such a thing as a unique, irreplaceable human element in education? If a machine is able to assign smart learning tasks, what is left for the teacher to do?

Along with constantly emerging new questions, we found that people answering these questions were often on opposite poles of the spectrum. One pole is that of a vocal opposition against digital technologies in the classroom. These people argue that the use of digital devices inhibits many of our brain functions, that teaching is, ultimately, a human endeavor, and advocates of education technology often don't know the first thing about education in general and how students learn in particular. The other pole is occupied by enthusiastic proponents of education technology and its limitless potential to advance human learning. People on this position are often entrepreneurs or like-minded individuals who attribute revolutionary potential to many digital technologies. They believe that learning can be made more efficient and fun through digital technology. Many people on the latter pole advocate for data-driven education, that is, the potential of machines to measure students to inform decisions about teaching, curricula, and, oftentimes, teacher assessments.

Our goal is to steer away from these poles in order to better understand the ultimate hard question itself. We will show that alarmism about education technology often romanticizes teaching, is sometimes ill-informed, and usually is unwarranted. We will also demonstrate that the alleged revolution of education is often nothing more than a mild reform advocated by people who are, indeed, not necessarily education experts but often programmers, salespeople, or venture capitalists who wish to do good with their insights and their capital. What we cannot do, however, is to give an all-encompassing view of the field. The mountains of research and the thousands of different streams in technological development are too numerous and too diverse to account for here, and others do that much better than we. Therefore, what follows are three theses summarizing our views on what constitutes large parts of the global hard question on education technology.

Overuse of Digital Devices

Thesis One: If we are not smart about their use in the classroom and beyond, students' vital cognitive functions could be damaged.

When we first brainstormed about this claim, we realized that none of us knew more than a few current telephone numbers of friends or family, and one didn't even know his own number. As we mentioned this to colleagues and friends, we realized it was no coincidence. While many could still remember phone numbers from their childhood, they knew barely any current ones. A full third of people under 30 tend to have problems recalling their own telephone number, and few of them can name their friends' numbers (Ian Robertson, personal communication, 2016). We can imagine many reasons unrelated to digital technology that would account for this. For instance, younger people change numbers more often than elderly people, who often have had the same landline number for decades. However, we clearly had to admit that we were simply prone to share our numbers through copy-pasting and reading them off our phone; in other words, digital technologies affected our motivation and ability to memorize.

This observation is well in line with authors such as Nicholas Carr who warn against an overuse of digital technology. Carr, author of *The Shallows—What the Internet is Doing to Our Brains* (2010), gained significant attention for warning against what he perceives as the danger of digital technology. Indeed, arguments of the Carr type—centered around changes in brain capacity and even physiology—are probably the most influential arguments on the side of digital skeptics. As Carr states in his Big Think talk titled *The Neuroscience of Internet Addiction*:

> I think there's a reason that a hundred years ago, when Rodin sculpted his great figure of the thinker, the thinker was in a contemplative pose and was concentrating deeply and wasn't multitasking. That is because, until recently anyway, this is something that people always thought was the deepest and most distinctly human way of thinking. That doesn't mean that I believe that all of us should sit in darkened rooms and think big thoughts without any stimuli coming at us all day. I think it's important to have a balance of those ways of thinking, but what the web seems to be doing—and a lot of the proponents of the web seem to be completely comfortable with—it's pushing us all in the direction of skimming and scanning and multitasking, and it's not encouraging us or even giving us an opportunity to engage in more attentive ways of thinking. (Carr, 2011)

When Carr and others warn of our loss in memory capacity, they run into a problem: the modern belief that memorizing facts isn't important anymore. Why should we know about the date of an historic event if the information is just a fingertip away? This argument has become particularly popular in education: We should stop teaching kids so much *knowledge* and instead foster *skills*, such as critical thinking and problem solving—the infamous 21st-century skills. Teaching mere facts has become a somewhat old-fashioned way of educating, reminding us of the 19th-century cliché of a lecturing schoolteacher. We believe that the modern disdain for teaching factual knowledge is exaggerated, and in order to make sense of the world, it is highly important to have a functioning memory.

Memorizing facts is not synonymous with senseless drilling of disconnected information. We need to amass knowledge to make sense of the world and to evolve as human beings. We cannot expect our students to think critically about texts and events they don't have foundational knowledge about, better known as context. It is a mistake to assume that factual knowledge and critical analysis are opposite poles. In truth, the latter is completely impossible without the former.

From a technical view of learning and understanding, it is clear that knowledge matters, but there is something more fundamentally important to knowing stuff: It is beautiful. Knowledge isn't purely functional. This might seem obvious, but many educational technology enthusiasts forget it.

One enthusiast educationalist and information technology scientist, Sugata Mitra, asks whether "it [is] necessary to learn new languages at all. Maybe machines will translate" (Matias, 2012). While such machines can be convenient, Professor Mitra ignores the power and the beauty of acquiring a new language. It is an enterprise that pushes our boundaries, lets us understand cultural differences, and enhances our view of the world. He and others who believe that knowledge is obsolete fail to understand that acquiring meaningful knowledge can be one of the most wonderful human experiences.

Due to the way we overuse digital media, we memorize fewer facts than our parents did. We also tend to process information in a shallower, more artificial way, and it has been shown that these effects are long term (Carr, 2010). Contrary to popular belief that knowing facts is outdated and shouldn't play a big role in education, it is actually as crucial to know stuff now as it was 100 years ago. The more facts we know, the easier it is to make sense of the world and to think critically. Finally, learning and knowing are too wonderful to outsource to machines.

The Dilemma of Digital Technologies

> Thesis Two: As digital technology can be harmful to some of our abilities, it will also train others, just as new technologies always have.

There is nothing new under the sun, and the belief that heavy use of communication technology is harmful to our brain and its functions is no exception. About 400 BC, Socrates expressed succinctly this concern:

> [. . .] this discovery of yours will create forgetfulness in the learners' souls because they will not use their memories; they will trust to the external written characters and not remember of themselves. The specific which you have discovered is an aid not to memory but to reminiscence. (Plato, orig. date unknown/1986)

Of course, Socrates wasn't referring to iPads, laptops, or the Class-Whizz. Socrates was talking about written language. He was concerned about two things: First, he believed that writing thoughts on paper meant a loss in meaning. A good philosopher and teacher, he said, would see writing as a negligible, playful activity, subpar to the vivid act of speaking. Second, he believed that written language created forgetfulness of the soul in the reader. A student should acquire wisdom by listening and speaking but not by reading texts. In our words, Socrates believed that written language causes a shallow way of interacting with information.

Fast-forward 2,400 years, and the argument has moved one step further: Books and articles are the medium of choice for philosophers and teachers, while the digital world is creating "forgetfulness in the soul, but just because the argument is old, it is not wrong. As we have seen, the ability to store information outside of our brain does indeed affects our ability to memorize. What neither Socrates nor today's skeptics see is that outsourcing of information, what some refer to a *transitional memory*, isn't a bad thing. If humans had listened to Socrates more, you wouldn't be benefitting from our insights today, and neither could we discuss Socrates' views today if his student Plato had not disregarded his teacher's disdain for written words. In a perhaps more benign dimension, would you be able to fully express the trains of thought in a successful term paper without referring to your writing? In short, while our ability to memorize might be affected, we can build, process, and use information better than Socrates could thanks to *transitional memory*.

While exploring this question in more detail, we came across three fundamental truths about human inventions from the wheel onwards. The first truth is that inventions make life more convenient. Instead of carrying heavy loads, the inventors of the wheel enabled us to put our baggage on a cart, and instead of having to know everything, the inventors of the microprocessor enabled us to retrieve information from Wikipedia, an expert on Reddit, or a saved PDF word list.

The second truth is that inventions can cause us to lose abilities. After humans became lazier and started to use the wheel for transportation, it seems conceivable that the late Bronze Age populations developed fitness deficits, and after the hard drive became an external source of information, we stopped remembering telephone numbers.

The third truth is that inventions make us develop new abilities. People quickly developed coordination and reflexes to drive horse wagons. Growing up digital means we will evolve to navigate the permanent connectedness and availability of information, and surely other, as yet unknown, skills will evolve (Stout, Toth, Schick, & Chaminade, 2008).

Indeed, there are impressive examples how young children—explorers and constructers by nature—can learn and use code to build new programs together with their peers. For instance, Scratch (Resnick et al., 2009), is a free blocks-based programming language developed by Mitch Resnick and colleagues at MIT with which students can not only create but also share their own interactive stories, games, and animations. Even some adults new to programming use it to get their first feel for the field. We found projects (Forsgren Velasquez et al., 2014) where Scratch is regularly used in primary school classes; children start with a simple base and are given a lot of time to tinker and show each other what they are accomplishing. Another case is that of a Chinese high school that one of us visited. Situated in the rural West of the country, few of its students ever make it to the nation's top colleges. In an attempt to enrich the limited education the students receive, the non-governmental organization called PEER conducted a Scratch boot camp that elicited enormous enthusiasm among the students. A quarter of the students, previously unexposed to programming, are now engaging in writing code. In a context where there is little opportunity to make it through conventional career paths, digital education technology not only taught fundamentally new skills, it also helped students navigate their way through a complex and demanding world.

All of these examples should be approached with more than the usual caution for one simple reason: We are talking about a new world entirely. The speed of the development in digital technologies is such that we have moved from *Tetris* to virtual reality headsets in 30 years. To rely on findings from today to predict what the digital space will do to us and for us in 30 years would be overreaching. It is, therefore, not only crucial to analyze the effect of current technologies but also to understand that extrapolations into the future are problematic. Henry Ford allegedly remarked that if he had asked people what they wanted, they would have asked for faster horses.

Humans will evolve and adapt to their technological surroundings, as they have done forever. While we might lose some abilities, we will also train other skills to cope with our environment. The endless opportunities of digital technologies are only beginning to unravel and can help us train some skills and brain functions more precisely than we could have done before. We have to identify and think about the best ways to use the available tools to educate and train ourselves. It would be unforgivable to remain in opposition to digital technologies in education and not use the power we have to learn and move forward. As the speed of technological development makes predictions hard, it is our job to grow with the machines and adapt constantly.

The Paradoxical Loop of New Technology: Moving Forward or Backwards?

Thesis Three: Existing education technology is far from revolutionary.

In most cases, we are dealing with digital textbooks and programs that are limited in their understanding of human learning. This causes the paradoxical loop that new technology actually leads us back to behaviorist modes of education of the 1950s. In the 1950s, Harvard psychologist B. F. Skinner built a device he called the teaching machine. Skinner was the most famous but not the first person to invent such a machine. Sidney Pressey had already designed a teaching machine in 1928. An early example of education technology enthusiasm, Skinner's teaching machine was an apparatus that fed a student columns of questions and, after the student had answered them, displayed the right answer. Skinner was one of the leaders of the psychological theory *behaviorism*. Behaviorist theory asserts, among other things, that learning happens largely due to the immediate consequences of our actions. If we experience rewards for behavior A and punishment for behavior B, so the theory goes, we will internalize behavior A and give up behavior B. Based on this theory, teachers and parents may praise children for doing good and may punish them for doing bad things. Similarly, Skinner's teaching machine was programmed to give students rewards for correct answers. The teaching machine also adapted to the student's progress and abilities. The better a student performed, the harder the subsequent questions and vice versa.

So what is wrong with this view of learning? Shouldn't we reward good behavior, and isn't education all about positive reinforcement? The problem is not that behaviorism is a false doctrine. The problem is that the way behaviorists understand learning is limited and can have adverse effects.

It seems evident that teaching is best when it instills profound interest in learning and exploring instead of using the proverbial carrot to condition children to display a certain behavior. Interest in learning and exploring, however, is harder to teach than a multiplication table. In particular, it is also harder to measure. This makes it wholly uninteresting to anyone who defines learning by giving unambiguous answers that are measured in a standardized test. Ironically, asking for unambiguous answers is much of what technology does, thereby reinforcing the current problematic notions of learning.

A simplified behaviorist understanding of learning is combined with the belief that quantitative data are great drivers of current education technologists. In the blunt words of Jose Ferreira, "A good tutor can crack jokes and make you want to learn, but this robot tutor can essentially read your mind" (Lapowsky, 2015). Jose Ferreira is the founder of Knewton, one of the biggest education technology enterprises in the world. It provides a digital tutoring system that gives the user an assignment and provides feedback about the solution. After the user answers questions, Knewton provides short explanatory videos about the topic at hand. Based on the user's performance, the prompts become more or less complex. This is not an exhaustive explanation of what Knewton does, but it is a significant part of its utility.

Now, see what happens when the mind-reading robot tutor is put to the test as one teacher did it (Tognoni, 2015). Let's assume we are a student and need to learn about algebraic expressions. Here is what Knewton provides: "If $x = -1$, what does $4(2x+1)$ equal?" If we make the common mistake of disregarding parentheses and going from left to right, our answer is $4 * -1 * 2 + 1 = -7$. Anyone who has ever taught mathematics, and even many who have not, will immediately understand how a student could reach this false conclusion. The teacher would then walk through the process with the student and tell him where he took the wrong turn, yet, no teacher would call this simple exercise reading your mind; rather she might call it doing her job. In contrast, what does the mind-reading robot tutor Knewton do? It simply states: "No, but keep trying."

Extrapolating from this example, we can say that the individualized, mind-reading robot tutor that took hundreds of millions of dollars and 7 years to design comes down to a flashier update of Skinner's teaching machine. A learner sits in front of a machine. The machine gives a prompt. The learner reacts. The machine affirms or denies. With such an understanding of learning, much of education technology isn't as much a mind-reading robot as it is a time machine to the 19th century.

Apart from the fact that current education technology isn't reading your mind when it comes to understanding math, it's naturally struggling even more when it needs to understand what makes you tick. Remember the study where kids were rewarded for playing math games? Most digital learning programs operate on exactly that premise: Solve a number of problems, and you can let a starship fire at an asteroid. Just as the parents who continuously bribe their children to make them obey, the computer doesn't know how counterproductive its teaching can be, and neither, at this point, do its programmers.

Education technology is no recent phenomenon, but it has evolved much less than its proponents believe. The grand promises about education technology overestimate what it is able to do at this point in time, as well as underestimate the human dimension of learning and teaching.

There are many aspects to good and successful learning. People selling education technology are largely catering to the behaviorist aspect of learning, not only a limited but sometimes a detrimental concept of learning.

BACK TO THE FUTURE

"Am I late again?" you wonder, calling up your watch. Blue letters light up on your right contact lens, calming you down: 8:45 a.m., plenty of time to get there before the first lesson. You decided to walk to school today as spring has set in, and a little morning exercise usually helps you focus during the day. Music in your ear, you don't hear your friend Jaime calling you from the other side of the street, so he runs over to greet you. You walk the rest of the way together, discussing math homework and sharing a sandwich. Math is your strongest subject. Mr. Khan has used the ClassWhizz system to assign you and some students from other grades a particularly challenging question: plan our new school hall.

As your school district is growing, more and more pupils are expected in the next years. After you researched and calculated the upcoming space demand by looking at the city's demographic projections, you went through various possible simulations of the new building. Mr. Khan helped your group to pay attention to important details. You went to several school events, observing movement patterns of the crowd, and met with the firefighters to put together recommendations about the location and the number of doors. You learned how sound behaves in differently shaped rooms and met with a local interior designer to learn about acoustic effects of different materials. Your group fed the specific information into ClassWhizz, and when meeting in virtual space in the last days, the simulations became better and better at mirroring what you knew every day. You can now express linear and basic logarithmic functions, calculate the volume of differently shaped solids, and are currently practicing and preparing the presentation of your recommendations for the upcoming town hall meeting.

Meanwhile, Jamie, who long thought he was not clever enough for math, has met with one of the school counselors. Like some of your classmates, he had avoided math for fear of failure. Under the guidance of Mr. Khan, your group received help with planning and also received math explanations from your group. Jamie doesn't like being lectured by teachers, let alone the ClassWhizz, but he is eager to learn when it is a peer doing the explaining. Just as each of your classmates, you have been coached as a mentor. The ClassWhizz math practice is so targeted at your own way of learning that you are now ahead of where students your age were a few decades ago; therefore, the school had no problem assigning many hours of mentoring training instead of core subjects.

When you talk to your parents, you have a hard time imagining their experiences of school. Their teachers must have known everything, given that they apparently told your parents most of what they know. You sometimes wonder whether teachers in the past were geniuses. Then again, your parents tell you how boring school often was. In your world, school might be hard work that you sometimes dodge in favor of soccer or reading, but it is rarely boring. Your classmates seem to think similarly. Your older teachers, such as Mr. Khan, still remember how often students wouldn't show up in the mornings. That rarely happens in your class, as there is usually important work to be done, and you don't want to let your friends down. As you are passing the gates to the schoolyard, you see Mr. Khan waving at you with his huge smile. You are happy to be here. You like school.

REFERENCES

Carr, N. (2010). *The Shallows. What the Internet is doing to our brains*. New York, NY: W.W. Norton and Co.

Carr, N. [Big Think] (2011, June 20). *The neuroscience of Internet addiction* [Video file]. Retrieved from https://www.youtube.com/watch?v=HjJYvLH_FGw

Forsgren Velasquez, N., Fields, D. A., Olsen, D., Martin, H. T., Strommer, A., Shepherd, M. C., & Kafai, Y. B. (2014). Novice programmers talking about projects: What automated text analysis reveals about online Scratch users' comments. In *Proceedings of the Annual Hawaii International Conference on System Sciences (HICSS)*. Waikoloa, Hawaii. IEEE.

Lapowsky, I. (2015, August 26). This robot tutor will make personalizing education easy. *Wired*. Retrieved from https://www.wired.com/2015/08/knewton-robot-tutor/

Matias, J. N. (2012, May 16). *Is education obsolete? Sugata Mitra at the MIT lab* [Blog post]. Retrieved from https://civic.mit.edu/blog/natematias/is-education-obsolete-sugata-mitra-at-the-mit-media-lab

Plato. (orig. date unknown /1986). *Phaedrus* (p. 123). Warminster, UK: Aris & Phillips.

Resnick, M., Maloney, J., Monroy-Hernandez, A., Rusk, N., Eastmond, E., Brennan, K.,..., & Kafai, Y. (2009). Scratch: Programming for all. *Communications of the ACM, 52*(11), 60–67.

Robertson, I. (2016) Personal communication.

Stout, D., Toth, N., Schick, K., & Chaminade, T. (2008). Neural correlates of Early Stone Age toolmaking: Technology, language and cognition in human evolution. *Philosophical Transactions of the Royal Society B: Biological Sciences, 363*(1499), 1939–1949. http://doi.org/10.1098/rstb.2008.0001

Tognoni, C. (2015, September 17). *Knewton knows knothing about my mind*. Retrieved from http://betteroffedu.com/post/129288891629/knewton-knows-knothing-about-my-mind

CHAPTER 7

Can Schools Prepare Kids for Work?

Love Basillote, Terence Tan Wei Ting, and Sharon Yoo

It's a bright, sunny day in Cambridge, Massachusetts, without a cloud in sight, but everyone's head is down, rushing from one class to the next as students think about the end of the year. With assignments due, final papers to write, and exams to take, all are unimpressed by the gorgeous spring day. On top of graduation requirements, most graduates are wondering about their job prospects: Will I find a job in line with my purpose that also gives me a reasonable financial return to my educational investment?

On the other side of the Charles River, employers are optimistic about the upswing in the economy. Businesses are slowly but surely recovering, and jobs are being created. For the first time since the crash of 2008, it seems that businesses are again feeling confident of their competitiveness. A cloud hanging over their heads, however, is the difficulty of finding qualified talent to sustain the fragile recovery and growth. Employers know that competitiveness will only be maintained with a strong human capital base. However, schools have been graduating students who are underqualified for the needs of the economy, as suggested by a recent report stating that job openings are outpacing hiring (Jamrisko, 2015).

We look at this picture and are puzzled that this is happening at a time when more investments are pouring into education globally. Initiatives like Education for All (EFA), a global education movement led by the United Nations Educational Scientific and Cultural Organization (UNESCO), are pushing societies to educate all children to improve human capital and spur growth. The share of education in developing countries' gross domestic product (GDP) thus continues to rise to meet international treaty obligations and increased demand for education within states. The business sector, led by traditional philanthropists and nouveau tech elites, is also pouring money into education. In the United States, it is estimated that each corporate donor allocated 17% of donations (equal to $14.4 million) in 2012 to K–12 education. All of these investments are made with potential returns in mind. For developing countries, education is supposed to be an engine for growth. For developed countries, education is seen as a tool to boost industry competitiveness. People invest in education with economic returns in mind—a livelihood for employees and productive workers for employers.

We know from recent history what happens when systems fail to prepare kids for work. High youth unemployment rates in the context of noninclusive growth have led to social unrest in many societies, particularly in the Middle East and North African (MENA) regions, toppling dictatorships and threatening fledgling democracies. When the social inequality that education supposedly addresses has been made worse, societies are left frustrated, and economies stagnate. In fact, the notion of *waithood* wherein youth are in a prolonged state of joblessness and limbo, waiting for an uncertain future, is now a modern phenomenon in some North African societies (Honwana, 2014).

Compounding the issue of failure of schools to prepare kids for work is the reality of a rapidly changing world, mainly due to technological and climatic shifts. The threat of climate change requires different skill sets for a society to be resilient. New technologies will mean that people will be able to hold on to their jobs longer but may face the threat of displacement by the very same technology that allows them to work at a much older age.

Indeed, change is a double-edged sword. While more jobs will be created, demand for skills will not only increase but also fundamentally change. Technology is threatening to replace people in the workplace. While people are able to work longer, the threat of skill irrelevance is looming. The reality is that the 12-year-olds of today will be working in jobs that do not yet exist (World Economic Forum, 2016). Millennials will go through seven to eight career changes—not jobs, but careers. Education that adequately prepared millions for 20th-century economies is now being put to the test as we move to an increasingly uncertain 21st century. The challenge of ensuring adequate educational preparation for an uncertain future is something that school systems need to confront.

Arguably, this is not new. However, the 21st-century economy will have serious implications for how school systems are designed and how education is delivered. It is a commonly held belief that having an education will make or break one's chances to take part in the world's prosperity. The failure of schools to prepare kids, especially from disadvantaged groups, for work not only sets them on a socioeconomic slow lane, it could accelerate their ultimate exclusion. As a global society, we cannot afford to ignore the education and economy nexus.

In this chapter, we try to make sense of the question "Can schools prepare kids for work?" in the context of a rapidly changing world, where more wealth is generated, investment in education is on the rise, and there is an increasing perception of the failure of education systems to equip kids with the skills to access the opportunities of a growing global economy. As a caveat, we acknowledge that it would be a disservice to education reform discourse to argue that the sole purpose of schools is to create a talent pipeline to support industries. Many, if not all, agree that there are other purposes to education. However, when jobs go unfilled while educated people are unemployed, there is a pressing need for schools to equip students with the skills and the competencies to be productive global citizens.

This question will be answered by looking at selected education systems in terms of how successful they are at preparing kids for work as indicated by youth unemployment, societal valuation and prioritization of career tracks, and employer-employee satisfaction. The choice of systems is both a pragmatic approach to existing literature, our professional experience, and guidance from experts. To push the conversation further, in succeeding sections we ask:

- How can we ensure that schools equip students with the right skills and competencies to be productive and fulfilled individuals?
- How can we design schools to become agents of equity and social justice by enabling kids to take part in the growth being generated?
- How do we make meaningful partnerships that truly serve learners and society as a whole?
- What are the factors that stop systems from preparing kids for work?

Three recommendations are offered on global education and work alignment for the consideration of policymakers, educators, and business leaders. We conclude with some reflections moving forward.

ARE SCHOOLS PREPARING KIDS FOR WORK?

Although education systems are intrinsically complex and vary from country to country, we offer three measures indicative of work preparedness: youth unemployment, diversity of pathways, and satisfaction of employers.

- *Youth unemployment* is defined as young people aged 15 to 24 who do not have a job but are actively looking for employment, education, or training (NEET) (Organization of Economic Cooperation and Development [OECD], 2016). It is an indication of one of two things: either a deficit of jobs due to an economic recession or a sign that the skills that youth gain from school are insufficient or incompatible for employment.
- *Diversity of pathways* looks at the supply side—whether education systems provide students with a range of appealing, high-quality postsecondary options after graduating from high school. The flexibility of an education system to satisfy different student demands and abilities is suggestive of strong school to work alignment.
- *Satisfaction of employers* looks at the demand side—whether employers think that their new hires are ready to cope with the responsibilities of the job. It is a good measure of how prepared graduates are for their chosen career and whether the skill expectations of employers are being met.

When looking further into these measures, there is reason to be pessimistic. Around the world, we are inadequately preparing our students for the world of work.

Youth Unemployment

Simply put, global unemployment is three times higher for youth than for adults. In fact, in 2015 Greece and Spain had youth unemployment rates higher than 50%; averaging 34% and 24%, respectively, over the previous 15 years. In contrast, the corresponding adult unemployment rates stood at 14% and 15%, respectively (World Bank, 2016). The situation is not much better closer to home. The national youth unemployment rate in the United States reached a high of 12% in mid-2015, placing 6.7 million youth out of school and out of work. This constitutes merely a fraction of the 76 million youth globally who face unemployment—more than a third of youth worldwide (Mejia et al., 2015).

Characteristically, the education systems in the countries mentioned above fail to provide all students appropriate preparation for the world of work. Greece's higher education sector is in a precarious situation. In 2013, austerity measures forced universities to lay off staff, causing the temporary shutdown of universities across the country (Smith, 2013). Even in the United States, states with policies to help students achieve workplace readiness face much lower unemployment rates than states without such policies. For example, Massachusetts has some of the best scores on standardized exams and also has alternative learning institutions such as the Farm School and North Star Initiative, and the GDP per capita for the state is $61,032 (Bureau of Economic Analysis, 2016). The same is true in other developed countries such as Sweden and the United Kingdom.

Meanwhile, in growing economies such as the Philippines, South Africa, and India, youth unemployment is persistent at 16.4%, 52.6%, and 10.4%, respectively (World Bank, 2016). It is interesting to note that in these three societies alternative pathways are discouraged or altogether nonexistent.

Diversity of Pathways

More often than not, we hear students gripe that society has a narrow range of mostly white-collar career expectations, and the route to these careers inevitably involves going to college. This is an international phenomenon—the assumption that the most reputable, highest-paying jobs rely on academic knowledge taught in colleges. This prioritization signals what celebrated educator Sir Ken Robinson calls a *knowledge hierarchy*: valuing one form of educational attainment over another (Robinson & Aronica, 2010; K. Robinson, personal communication, March 2, 2016). In most countries, academic knowledge is pervasively considered more rigorous and a better guarantee of success than vocational knowledge. This could leave youth disempowered if they pursue career tracks based on their personal interests.

By streaming or tracking students into certain career paths regardless of interest or capabilities, education systems leave them disengaged and often disillusioned. In the United States, the education system is foremost designed to stream students into tertiary education, with limited consideration for alternative vocational pathways. In fact, 69.2% of all high school graduates enroll in college or university (Bureau of Labor Statistics, 2015). This alone might not send a strong signal that college is the only way to a good job, but it doesn't stop there. Vocational tracks in high schools have little cachet—they are under-resourced, ill equipped, and have low student expectations. Minorities, children from low-income families, and academic laggards are disproportionately represented (Oakes, 2005). Moreover, the preference of a college path can be observed all over the country, with high schools promoting pre-collegiate programs such as Advanced Placement and International Baccalaureate Diploma, programs sought after by college admissions managers.

In conjunction with the knowledge hierarchy, educational systems signal the value they place on academia through high-stakes examinations required to enter universities. Examples can be seen in countries such as India, Korea, and the United States, where one exam determines a student's future. Given the highly competitive college admissions process of these systems, perversions occur. Allegations of cheating and teaching to the test are rampant. The outcome is that kids become good at taking exams rather than actually gaining skills needed to be successful in life. Moreover, recent research questions whether these tests are good indicators of college persistence and success, given the high psychological strain on students and families.

In Korea, the score on the exit exam or College Scholastic Ability Test sets the career and social trajectory for the rest of a student's life, including employment, marriage, and societal standing. The top universities or SKY universities only accept the top scorers. According to former president, Lee Myung-bak, only 1% of students taking the exam achieve these scores. In India, top colleges such as St. Stephen's College of Delhi University only accept students scoring 96.5% or above on their Central Board of Secondary Education or Indian Certificate of Secondary Education final examinations (The Press Trust of India, 2015). The Indian Institute of Technology also has the Joint Entrance Exam, taken by 1.2 to 1.5 million applicants per yea, in addition to their high school exit exams, with an acceptance rate of 2% (Mayyasi, 2013). Acceptance in elite U.S. institutions is similarly competitive. Top schools such as Harvard and Stanford have acceptance rates of around 5%. SAT or ACT scores are highly correlated to admission in selective institutions.

When education systems create high-stakes standardized tests and tracking mechanisms to control and limit access to higher education, they exacerbate the knowledge hierarchy and disincentivize alternate postsecondary options, such as vocational education. The result? Students accept the paradigm that college is the only pathway to a well-paying job and overlook valuable alternative pathways that might be a better fit for them.

Satisfaction of Employers

The perception that employers have of new graduate hires ranges from ambivalent to pessimistic. According to a McKinsey report on *Education to Employment*, nearly 4 in 10 companies with entry-level job openings in the nine countries surveyed were unable to fill these vacancies because of a skills shortage among graduates. The same report found that only 42% of employers believe that new participants to the labor force are prepared to join the workforce. This skepticism about the competence of graduates means that employers need to offer new-hire training; 84% of companies train for general skills that graduates lack, while 90% train for job-specific skill sets.

The mismatch between employer expectation and graduate competence can be summarized in a set of four challenges facing new graduates (Candy & Crebert, 1991; Crebert et al., 2004):

1. How to apply theories, principles, and information learned at school to work-related responsibilities.
2. How to cope with aspects of the workplace such as problem solving, decision making, working in a team, and independent learning.
3. How to break away from the expectations of close supervision, order, and control that exist within college but not at work.
4. How to move from the familiar, structured learning approaches adopted in college to self-reflective learning aimed at change and self-development.

These challenges reflect the impressions of employers when asked about new hires. In Australia, for instance, employers felt that new graduates had inflated expectations of starting salaries and development opportunities, and they were inadequately prepared to make decisions or work in teams (Crebert et al., 2004).

However, employers were more satisfied with their new hires in certain situations. The level of employer satisfaction is higher in large companies with 500 or more employees because these firms often put a concerted effort into talent selection and are able to hire the best graduates (AC Nielsen, 2000). Also, employers reported that work placement opportunities were effective in moderating the expectations that students had about work (Crebert et al., 2004), which led to greater satisfaction towards these employees.

Slivers of Hope

Although many global education systems seem bleak, there are pockets of dynamic systems worldwide that are supporting students experiencing cohesive transition into the workforce. In many cases, countries invest in national-scale programs to change the societal paradigm by investing in youth education and skills. Countries in Europe, such as Switzerland and Germany, have traditionally featured apprenticeship models, which heavily invest in the development of young talent through strong social partnerships. In these systems, companies in various industries train students in real-world skills while they are still in school. Commonly known as dual-training models, apprenticeships happen in conjunction with secondary schooling for specific professions and vocations.

In Switzerland, watch-making companies such as Swatch Group and the Federation of Swiss Watch Manufacturers have created apprenticeship models that work in conjunction with traditional schooling. Similar dual systems exist in many countries such as Germany and Austria with Technical Vocational and Educational Training Programs (TVET); Egypt with Mubarak Kohl Initiative Interventions, which guarantees employment after training; and China, which recently adopted a dual-track program similar to Germany's.

Other than apprenticeship models, Finland has incorporated an interdisciplinary method called phenomenon-based learning (similar to problem-based learning) that approaches learning through projects incorporating various disciplines such as math, science, and technology. The ideology is to produce simulated versions of professional workplace environments.

Even already thriving education systems are constantly renewing themselves to better prepare children for the vocations they will be assuming. After experimenting with apprenticeships in the 1970s and 1980s, Singapore's Institutes of Technical Education (ITE) chose in the 1990s to approach vocational education from a very different perspective than the time-honored models of Western Europe. ITE closely collaborated with industry partners to build realistic models of working environments, called the *factory school*. Mechanics-in-training worked on Nissan and Suzuki cars and special cutaway engines built to exacting specifications, while hospitality students served real guests at a hotel located on the ITE campus.

In the early years of the millennium, the leaders of ITE realized that this was not enough. Their intimate connection to government and industry, a partnership that has been enshrined in policy and practice since the 1960s, allowed them to realize that the future, even for vocational students, lay in high-value-added niche industries. Accordingly, the ITEs introduced training for careers as specific as biotech laboratory technicians, digital animators, and performing arts technicians. At the same time, faculty were required to contribute to their respective sectors by participating in professionally relevant industry projects. This system, called Do or Lead, ensures that ITE instructors remain relevant and up to date about the issues surrounding their industry. Ultimately, for the ITEs, and for the students under their care, synchronizing the world of school to the world of work pays off.

With flexible and relevant school-to-work pipelines and social partnerships, Singapore's youth unemployment is relatively low at 9.6% and total unemployment is even lower at 1.2% (Ministry of Manpower, 2016). This number can be partially attributed to ITE taking a group of youths who might not do so well in an academic learning environment and giving them the best hands-on learning that money can buy.

CAN SCHOOLS PREPARE STUDENTS FOR WORK?

Our research has brought us to the conclusion that schools can prepare kids for work. As seen in the previous section, there are isolated pockets of success across the globe. A better question to ponder, perhaps, is: "How can schools prepare kids for work?" Successful examples of school-to-work transitions, both nationally and globally, have one element in common: they collaborate extremely closely with employers and policymakers. This drives to the heart of how schools can best prepare their students for the world of work.

The only way to prepare our kids for the workplace is by realizing that the responsibility of education does not fall solely on the school. Indeed, the best partnerships between policymakers, education, and business achieve better student outcomes than merely placing the responsibility on any one sector alone (Wang, 2012). We call this form of collaboration *empowered partnerships* to emphasize the unique, essential role that each sector plays in enabling the others towards a common goal: ensuring that our children graduate fully prepared for work (Figure 7.1).

Leaving out any one sector can lead to suboptimal outcomes. Schools and employers working together in the absence of policymakers can lead to fragile, even tense, relations (Rivkin, 2014). Governmental intervention can serve to mediate conflicting priorities. When employers and policymakers join forces and leave schools out, there are often

Figure 7.1. Collaboration Empowerment Partnership

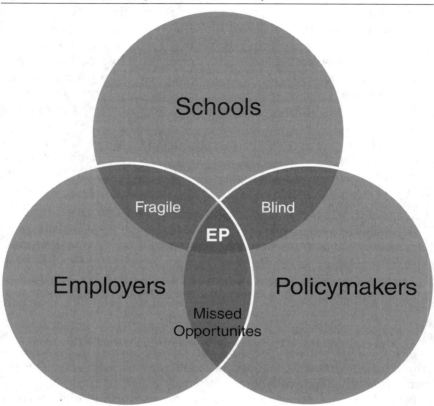

missed opportunities to use existing educational frameworks to prepare youths for work, resulting in duplication of infrastructure, and when governmental bodies and schools work directly on career readiness without engaging employers, they are essentially operating blind without direct input from the very organizations in which the youths will be working.

Empowered partnerships surveyed for this research seek to reform the current school-to-career pipeline in a number of ways. Although describing these reforms in detail is out of the scope of this chapter, there are three broad principles that undergird many of these. Notably, the failure of these principles to gain further traction—that is, the difficulties in applying them at scale—reveal how tension between sector players can and have jeopardized empowered partnerships.

1. Multiple Pathways—Career and Technical Education (CTE)

Bob Schwartz, head of the Pathways to Prosperity network at the Harvard Graduate School of Education, is doubtful that traditional 4-year colleges are the gateway to well-paying, rewarding jobs for all. "In recent years, we've seen a pushback against the assumption that we should strive towards college for all. The high cost of tuition, mounting student debt, a diminished return on investment for each year of college—all these are causing students in the United States to look for opportunities outside 4-year colleges" (Schwartz, personal communication, March 22, 2016). Instead, Schwartz advocates a multiple pathways approach: building alternative postsecondary education tracks to complement 4-year colleges and linking these alternative pathways closely to the requirements of individual jobs or vocational sectors (Symonds, Schwartz, & Ferguson, 2011).

Doing so has clear advantages besides the mounting costs of 4-year colleges. The best alternative pathways, including career and technical education (CTE) programs, build on a unique blend of hands-on experiential learning and classroom theory, designed in close collaboration with industry. These programs are attractive to students who might not maximize their potential in a formal classroom setting and who perform best with pedagogy that emphasizes application. Unsurprisingly, the best programs feature committed, empowered partnerships between policymakers, schools, and employers.

Policymakers. Depending on the degree of influence policymakers can exert on educational systems, their contribution towards a multiple pathways approach can take different forms. If their influence is more indirect, as in the United States, policymakers can foster high-quality CTE programs by coordinating efforts between employers and schools. This is what Massachusetts did when four Workforce Development Boards within the state saw a need to connect employers in the manufacturing sector to skilled workers (Robin Dion, personal communication, April 11, 2016). Pooling resources, they applied for a grant to set up the Northeast Advanced Manufacturing Consortium (NAMC), an industry-led partnership to "promote sustained collaborations between industry, academic, and workforce development". NAMC currently works with more than 90 member companies, three community colleges, and a number of vocational-technical schools within the northeast Massachusetts region to provide high school graduates with quality vocational education, with attractive remuneration and employment prospects.

If policymaking is centralized, the role of the policymaker turns from arbiter to leader: from managing collaboration to playing a much more assertive role. International exemplars of the multiple pathways approach often feature governments with the institutional and political wherewithal to play an active role in sponsoring high-quality CTE programs. The much praised apprenticeship model in Switzerland is regulated and steered by the federal government, which works closely with industry associations to define vocational training curricula and standards for each sector (Hoffman & Schwartz, 2015). Singapore's Institutes of Technical Education were set up in 1992 with a $300 million capital investment by the government, have dedicated waves of 5-year plans to assure its continued evolution, and leaders were drafted from economic policy-planning units. In each case, policymakers were able to play a leadership role in guiding the educational trajectory and inclusion of CTE programs.

Employers. A multiple pathways approach to education requires the enthusiastic participation of employers because one of the biggest selling points of alternative postsecondary pathways, including CTE programs, is its close relationship to industry. Says Robin Dion, the Manufacturing Marketing Manager of NAMC, "The placement rate upon graduating from our training programs is more than 90%, and the only way we can guarantee this is by ensuring that companies are happy with our training programs" (personal communication, April 11, 2016). Involving employers within the planning of CTE curricula makes explicitly clear what skills and competencies students will be trained in. This minimizes the signaling problem facing many degree holders—employers know that you have a degree, but they are unsure exactly what skills you have (Mourshed, Farrell, & Barton, 2013).

Getting employers involved is most crucial in the curriculum development process, where schools are deciding what to include in a CTE program. Many empowered partnerships feature employers looking closely at the jobs they need fulfilled, the responsibilities required, and the skills required to satisfy the responsibilities. They then enter into a conversation with schools as to how these skills can be best taught in a classroom setting and how to assess them. The Automotive Manufacturing Training and Education Collective (AMTEC), for instance, draws upon high-performing technicians who work daily on the shop floor to identify key tasks they performed and the competencies for each task. These are collectively distilled with schools into 60 study modules, each lasting from 3 to 8 weeks (Mourshed et al., 2013). Employers in empowered partnerships also provide opportunities for students in CTE programs to gain authentic learning experiences within the company.

In the Swiss and German dual-education systems, employers welcome and expect students to take up apprenticeships as part of their CTE program, often in a company for which they end up working (Hoffman & Schwartz, 2015).

Schools. The contributions of K–12 schools to this particular principle are not as obvious compared to those of policymakers and employers, yet schools can embrace the multiple pathways approach by identifying students who might be interested or who might best benefit from a CTE program instead of 4-year college. "We work with the teachers and the counselors from Cambridge Rindge and Latin School to identify students who have no plans after high school as of yet, and we target this group directly in our marketing," Dion tells us (personal communication, April 11, 2016). Recognizing that some students would benefit more from a CTE program reduces the stigma and the negative impressions that students and parents often get from such programs.

Some schools go one step further and adopt alternative pathways themselves, which are often more CTE-focused. These schools have many of the features of high-quality CTE programs, such as close industry collaborations and strong government support, with two key differences. First, students start vocational training earlier, as young as 14; second, the door is clearly left wide open for graduates to pursue further qualifications such as a college degree. Pathways in Technology Early College High School (P-TECH), in Brooklyn, New York, is an example of such a school. Despite collaborating closely with IBM and ensuring that all graduates receive an associate's degree, the school's guidance counselors take pains to highlight the possibility of attaining a college degree after graduation. Although the entire graduating cohort of 2015 received job offers from IBM, four students chose to go on to 4-year colleges (Golod, 2015). This flexibility and the permeability between educational tracks is crucial so that these early-stage CTE programs do not end up constraining students' aspirations.

2. Career Counselling

Writers from Howard Gardner to Ken Robinson are emphasizing the importance of helping students find career pathways that, in Gardner, Csikszentmihalyi, and Damon's (2002) words, are "excellent, engaging, and ethical," yet encouraging students to pursue careers for which they are suited—and showing them how to get there—is easier said than done. Internationally, many students report not finishing school because they don't see the point in continued schooling; even for those who do, many make uninformed choices that they may up regretting (Mourshed et al.,

2013). For the authors, our senior year of high school experiences were collectively dominated by a narrow range of career ambitions such as becoming a doctor, lawyer, or a civil servant. Many of our peers in elite careers are now considering a career switch. Making information about different career pathways available and transparent to low-income and minority students can open up a range of ambitions to these students previously considered impossible or solely the domain of a privileged class.

Policymakers. As the sector with access to macro-level data about economic and educational trends, policymakers are in a unique position to condense this data and present it in an accessible format to students and their parents. Data of interest include information about graduate starting salaries, number of available jobs in each industry for the upcoming year, and historical data on career and employment prospects for the different postsecondary qualifications. This constitutes vital information for students and parents to consider when deciding on a career track, yet is not often made available.

There are three aspects to this as a policy move. First, merely presenting data that existed previously only in the archives of government statisticians already goes a long way to increase transparency. Second, presenting the data in an accessible, interactive, and intuitive way, similar to what Data USA has done for public data, would allow parents and students to make meaningful comparisons between career pathways. Finally, it would also debunk the myth that 4-year colleges represent the pathway to the best-paying jobs in all industries. Although they come from different backgrounds, Dion and Schwartz are emphatically unambiguous on this point: for many careers, CTE programs provide a better return on investment than traditional colleges.

By being provided with a fuller picture of different careers and educational tracks, students and parents can make a more informed choice. For instance, the Colombia Labor Observatory provides highly detailed labor market information on its website, disaggregating information down to the level of the individual school (Mourshed et al., 2013). Students and parents can not only dive into the graduation and employment rates of every postsecondary institution in the country, but they can also track this data longitudinally, following a cohort over time. This is a powerful tool for students choosing between a plethora of options after graduating from high school.

Employers. Instead of data, the employers researched provide a very different type of information to students looking to make career choices:

the indispensable experience of working within the company. These exposure programs include field placements, internships, and company visits and expose students to the company culture, the work of the company, and, more broadly, to the experience of working in the industry. This provides students with a more realistic expectation about various career tracks and can also help to disabuse students of stereotypes and expectations of industries. For example, students and parents in North Carolina who attended a factory visit organized by Siemens were surprised to find that the plant featured high-tech equipment and modern manufacturing technologies instead of the dirty, dangerous conditions that had made them think twice about working in a factory (Mourshed et al., 2013).

The best exposure programs that allow students to actively engage with authentic problems and contribute to the company are, unsurprisingly, more meaningful than other programs. At the same time, employers approach exposure programs through a developmental lens, understanding that students are continually growing with their work experience. To this end, many work with their interns to set both learning and professional goals for the exposure program.

At P-TECH, for example, rising seniors are given the opportunity to intern at IBM offices over the summer. They are placed within research teams and work on real-world assignments before finally presenting their work to an audience including IBM board members and P-TECH faculty (Golod, 2015). In the U.K., JPMorgan partners with the Social Mobility Foundation to bring low-income students to London for summer internships where they assume revenue-generating roles and connect with JPMorgan mentors (JPMorgan Chase, 2016). Both IBM and JPMorgan's exposure programs overwhelmingly benefit low-income, minority students; providing the opportunity to work in global powerhouses such as these is a powerful esteem-building measure that boosts career aspirations.

Schools. Schools have traditionally assumed the role of advisor to students unsure about career pathways, and they have done so in one of two ways. Comprehensive career counselling is one such way, and countries such as Japan, Norway, Finland, and Switzerland have successfully embedded career planning within the school curriculum. In Swiss career planning classes, for instance, all students learn about the various occupations, typical working hours, and the vocational or academic training path for each (Mourshed et al., 2013). P-TECH students have access to three guidance counselors and assistant principals on hand to provide advice on postgraduation prospects (Golod, 2015). Bolting on career counselling in this way seems to be the most popular approach internationally, and it has yielded positive returns in some cases.

The main obstacle to this approach, at least in the case of the United States, is that the resources currently devoted to career counseling are inadequate for this sort of curriculum-embedded career counselling. Counselors in school have an average caseload of about 479 students, way above the 250 to 1 ratio recommended by the American School Counselor Association (Association for Career and Technical Education [ACTE], 2008). Due to a lack of adequate training during counselor preparation programs, many career counselors are inadequately prepared to advise students on career and educational planning (ACTE, 2008).

An alternative to this strategy of bolting on career counseling to existing systems is to build in career exposure within individual academic classes. Such initiatives would make the real-world relevance of their coursework unequivocally clear, as well as allow students to directly experience the problem-solving approaches that characterize different vocations. While not necessarily for K–12 students, seniors in Olin College, for example, work directly with major institutions from the public and private sectors—from NGOs to Fortune 500 firms—on a senior capstone project, providing innovative solutions to real-world problems (Olin College of Engineering, 2016). Similar approaches in the K–12 sector are rarer, but examples from institutions such as High Tech High provide insights as to how students can collaborate with industry professionals to solve genuine problems. A team from High Tech High Chula Vista created a community rideshare website using Drupal, an open source website building software, with generous face-to-face and online advice from tech professionals who specialized in the software (McNamara, 2013). Many teachers in the High Tech High network are former industry professionals able to leverage their networks to bring in guest speakers, set up internships, and make explicit connections between classroom learning and real-life applications.

3. Uneven Outcomes: Soft Skills

Distinct from the technical expertise that CTE programs strive to develop, other researchers focus on the importance of portable, transferable skills increasingly important in today's knowledge-based economy. These skills go by many names: soft skills, 21st-century skills, and cross-disciplinary skills. Despite the label, these skills are in high demand. In Peru, socioemotional skills were particularly prized by employers, while in the Philippines, employers lamented the lack of candidates with valuable skills such as creativity, initiative, and leadership (UNESCO, 2012). It is becoming increasingly clear that the jobs of the future, whether in developing or developed countries, will require these skills, and those who possess them will stand at a competitive advantage. What is less clear is whether employers, policymakers, and schools have a cohesive plan for how to collectively develop these transferable skills or even a common description of what these skills are. Current tripartite collaboration to foster transferable skills falls short of being considered empowered partnerships.

Policymakers. Many states and countries have adopted some form of commitment to infusing transferable skills into teaching, with varying results. Singapore's Ministry of Education, for example, has made a concerted drive to infuse 21st-century competencies into the education system since its introduction in 2007. The highly centralized education system in Singapore meant that policymakers and curriculum developers could incorporate these 21st-century skills across the breadth of the entire schooling experience, from using technology in the classroom to character development (Liew, 2013). Even as this met with positive results and praise by external commentators such as Sir Michael Barber, local commentators found an inherent tension between the flexible, subjective 21st-century skills and Singapore's high-stakes testing regime (Davie, 2016).

The approach of policymakers in the United States towards transferable, 21st-century skills reflects a similar but more severe tension. On one hand, we see the Partnership for 21st-Century Learning (P21) encourage more states to become P21 leadership states (so far, 20 states have signed up) and more schools to become P21 exemplar schools, paragons of excellence for those looking to see how it looks when these skills are infused in classrooms (P21, 2016). On the other hand, we observe the rise of test-based accountability regimes to ensure that all students attain predetermined standards—what Sahlberg (2012) calls drily the Global Education Reform Movement, or GERM.

Employers. There is a collective call from employers worldwide for these transferable skills. For large companies such as Accenture, transferable skills are important given the sheer size of the organization and the required geographic and thematic mobility of its employees (Nanterme & Carmichael, 2015). Employees at large companies are expected to be team players, adaptive, proactive, and savvy in navigating both company culture and change. One could argue that the same set of skills is required for small companies and startups at the forefront of innovation. However, despite a shared need for these skills, employers can't seem to agree on what these skills actually look like.

For education systems to catch up with the speed and the breadth of change, employers would have to agree on the definition of these skills and be part of the conversation around standards setting. In successful countries such as Germany and Switzerland, employers are important players in curriculum settings. The concern raised by certain employers about possible talent poaching and specific skills as part of their trade secret will only leave everyone to stand to lose. In the case of Massachusetts, employers were part of the design of the curriculum that gives students the right set of skills and employers the kind of talent that will help their companies grow.

Schools. The disagreement on the definition of skills within business has inadvertently given schools mixed signals and has led to educators moving from one in-vogue set of skills to another. However, the blame cannot all be placed on business. It is also important for educators to reach out to employers within their localities and not perpetuate the idea that education exists within the realm of the classroom bubble, isolated from the real world.

Informed by business through engaged partnerships, further research could inform the pedagogy needed to better teach the skills that industry needs.

CONCLUSION

The question "Can schools prepare kids for work?" is complex. Therefore, this chapter is anchored on the following questions: "Why should this matter?" "What can we learn from experience?" and "What could a strong school-work system look like in the future?"

While emphasis is given to the sociocultural over the economic purpose of education in most higher education classes, there is substantial research, as well as many real-world examples, to back our claims that a strong focus on school to work can benefit today's students. Additionally, there is value in scholarly and practical dissent. On one hand, there is no certainty in future plans because things are yet to unfold. Specific recommendations might no longer be applicable in the very near future. On the other hand, generic suggestions can easily become irrelevant. Therefore, we chose to provide recommendations that could be applicable in various contexts, with specific points provided about the barriers that prevent systems from adequately preparing kids for work.

Ultimately, this question can mean different things to various individuals or groups. Focus can, therefore, change depending on one's perspective. However, a question this big cannot just be a task of one stakeholder or two. Therefore, we emphasize an engaged partnership approach and hope that this approach will guide the thinking of education systems designers and be one of the bridges connecting students and employers from both sides of the river.

REFERENCES

AC Nielsen Research, & Department of Education, Training and Youth Affairs, Australia. (2000). *Employer satisfaction with graduate skills: research report* (TD/TNC 62.120). Retrieved from VOCEDplus: http://www.voced.edu.au/content/ngv%3A13863

Association for Career and Technical Education (ACTE). (2008, December). *Career and technical education's role in career guidance.* Retrieved from https://www.acteonline.org/WorkArea/DownloadAsset.aspx?id=2095

Candy, P. C., & Crebert, R. G. (1991). Ivory tower to concrete jungle: The difficult transition from the academy to the workplace as learning environments. *The Journal of Higher Education, 62*(5), 570. doi:10.2307/1982209

Crebert, G., Bates, M., Bell, B., Patrick, C.-J., & Cragnolini, V. (2004). Ivory tower to concrete jungle revisited. *Journal of Education and Work, 17*(1), 47–70. doi:10.1080/1363908042000174192

Davie, S. (2016, January 19). Learning for life? Policies, parents need to change too. *The Straits Times.* Retrieved from http://www.straitstimes.com/opinion/learning-for-life-policies-parents-need-to-change-too

Gardner, H., Csikszentmihalyi, M., & Damon, W. (2002). *Good work: When excellence and ethics meet.* United States: Basic Books.

Golod, A. (2015, June 2). Proving P-TECH success: Students graduate with diploma and tech degree. *U.S. News.* Retrieved from http://www.usnews.com/news/stem-solutions/articles/2015/06/02/proving-p-tech-success-students-graduate-with-diploma-and-tech-degree

Hoffman, N., & Schwartz, R. (2015). *Gold standard: The Swiss vocational education and training system.* Retrieved from http://www.ncee.org/wp-content/uploads/2015/03/SWISSVETMarch11.pdf

Honwana, A. (2014). "Waithood": Youth transitions and social change. In D. Foeken, T. Dietz, L. Haan, & L. Johnson (Eds.), *Development and equity: An interdisciplinary exploration by ten scholars from Africa, Asia and Latin America* (pp. 28–40). Leiden, The Netherlands: Brill.

Jamrisko, M. (2015, June 9). *Job openings outpace hiring in U.S. for first time on record.* Retrieved from http://www.bloomberg.com/news/articles/2015-06-09/job-openings-in-u-s-rose-more-than-forecast-in-april

JPMorgan Chase & Co. (2016). *Building pathways to success.* Retrieved from https://www.jpmorganchase.com/corporate/Corporate-Responsibility/document/JPMC_NSFY_brochure_AW4_accessible.pdf

Liew, W. (2013). *Development of 21st century competencies in Singapore* [Power-Point slides]. Retrieved from https://www.oecd.org/edu/ceri/02%20Wei%20Li%20Liew_Singapore.pdf

Mayyasi, A. (2013, June 27). *The IIT entrance exam*. Retrieved from http://priceonomics.com/the-iit-entrance-exam/

McNamara, T. (2013). Solving real-world problems with open source software. *UnBoxed*. Retrieved from http://www.hightechhigh.org/unboxed/issue10/open_source_software/

Mejia, N., Perez-Arce, F., Lundberg, M., Munshi, F., Bangladesh, S. M., Rubio, & J. Solutions for Youth Employment (S4YE). (2015). *Toward solutions for youth employment: A 2015 baseline report*. Retrieved from http://www.ilo.org/wcmsp5/groups/public/---ed_emp/documents/publication/wcms_413826.pdf

Ministry of Manpower, Singapore. (2016, April 28). *Summary table: Unemployment*. Retrieved May 16, 2016, from Ministry of Manpower, http://stats.mom.gov.sg/Pages/Unemployment-Summary-Table.aspx

Mourshed, M., Farrell, D., & Barton, D. (2013). *Education to employment: Designing a system that works*. Retrieved from http://mckinseyonsociety.com/downloads/reports/Education/Education-to-Employment_FINAL.pdf

Nanterme, P., & Carmichael, S. (2015, December 3). *Accenture's CEO on leading change*. Retrieved from https://hbr.org/ideacast/2015/12/accentures-ceo-on-leading-change.html

Oakes, J. (2005). *Keeping track: How schools structure inequality* (2nd ed.). New Haven, CT: Yale University Press.

OECD. (2016). *Youth not in employment, education or training (NEET)* (indicator). doi: 10.1787/72d1033a-en

Olin College of Engineering. (2016, May 11). *Senior capstone program (SCOPE)*. Retrieved from Olin College of Engineering, http://www.olin.edu/collaborate/scope/

P21. (2016). *P21: Partnership for 21st century learning*. Retrieved from http://www.p21.org/index.php

The Press Trust of India. (2015, June 17). DU admissions: You need 99 per cent to study English at St Stephen's College. *The Indian Express*. Retrieved from http://indianexpress.com/article/india/india-others/2015-16-admissions-st-stephens-announces-first-cut-off-list-english-highest-at-99-per-cent/

Rivkin, J. (2014, February). *Partial credit: How America's school superintendents see business as a partner*. Retrieved from http://www.hbs.edu/competitiveness/Documents/partial-credit.pdf

Robinson, K., & Aronica, L. (2010). *The element: How finding your passion changes everything*. London, UK: Penguin Books.

Sahlberg, P. (2012, June 30). *How GERM is infecting schools around the world*. Retrieved from http://pasisahlberg.com/text-test/

Smith, H. (2013, September 25). Austerity measures push Greek universities to point of collapse. *The Guardian*. Retrieved from http://www.theguardian.com/world/2013/sep/25/austerity-measures-push-greek-universities-collapse

Symonds, W., Schwartz, R., & Ferguson, R. (2011, February). *Pathways to prosperity: Meeting the challenge of preparing young Americans for the 21st century*. Cambridge, MA: Pathways to Prosperity Project, Harvard University Graduate

School of Education. Retrieved from https://dash.harvard.edu/bitstream/handle/1/4740480/Pathways_to_Prosperity_Feb2011-1.pdf?sequence=1

UNESCO. (2012). *Youth and skills: Putting education to work.* Retrieved from http://unesdoc.unesco.org/images/0021/002180/218003e.pdf

U.S. Department of Commerce, Bureau of Economic Analysis. (2016, March 24). *Massachusetts.* Retrieved from https://bea.gov/regional/bearfacts/pdf.cfm?fips=25000&areatype=STATE&geotype=3

U.S. Department of Labor, Bureau of Labor Statistics. (2016, May 12). *College enrollment and work activity of 2015 high school graduates.* Retrieved from http://www.bls.gov/news.release/hsgec.nr0.htm

Wang, Y. (2012, January). *Education in a changing world: Flexibility, skills, and employability.* Retrieved from http://www-wds.worldbank.org/external/default/WDSContentServer/WDSP/IB/2012/05/23/000356161_20120523022400/Rendered/PDF/691040WP00PUBL0ability0WEB050110120.pdf

World Bank. (2016). *Unemployment, youth total (% of total labor force ages 15–24)* (modeled ILO estimate). Retrieved from http://data.worldbank.org/indicator/SL.UEM.1524.ZS

World Economic Forum. (2016). *The future of jobs employment, skills and workforce strategy for the fourth industrial revolution.* Retrieved from http://www3.weforum.org/docs/WEF_Future_of_Jobs.pdf

CHAPTER 8

Can Higher Education Be Transactional?

Zachary Goldman, Wen Qiu, and Randy Tarnowski

Looking back on our own experiences in higher education and towards future steps personally and professionally, we continue to reflect upon what we have gained from this experience of researching and writing about a hard question regarding global education. As we visited the career services office, updated each other on job interviews, and passed along cover letter tips, we realized that we shared the same, terrifying question: What is my degree actually worth?

Being students in a graduate school of education, we were a bit unsettled. Shouldn't education be a priceless, transformative experience? Is it even right to think about higher education from an investment/return perspective? We all agree with Dr. Muriel A. Howard, president of American Association of State Colleges and Universities (AASCU), who has argued that universities help students discover their individuality, their place in the world, and their unique aptitudes (Howard, 2013). Similarly, we affirm William Cronon's claim in his 1998 essay that a liberal education is about gaining the power, the wisdom, the generosity, and the freedom to connect (Cronon, 1998). We see education as an experience of personal transformation in the service of the public good.

However, as students from the United States and China, we also realize that, together, we have spent over $460,000, in addition to need-and merit-based scholarships and grants, on our respective undergraduate and graduate degrees. Much of this is in the form of loans, which we will be paying back, with interest, for the foreseeable future. We are certainly not alone. According to the Institute of College Access and Success, 69%

of those who graduated from public or nonprofit colleges in 2014 had student loan debt, with an average of nearly $29,000 per student. In fact, the week before commencement, a small plane circled our city trailing a sign that promoted the refinancing of student loans. Considering that many students end up in debt and leave school without completing a college degree, we are grateful for graduating and for having attended a highly selective institution. Most students with similar levels of debt aren't so lucky.

Higher education is often thought of as an extra service to which not everyone is entitled. This is a key difference between this chapter and previous ones, which are focused largely on compulsory and publicly funded K–12 education. Typically, people are only able to choose to pursue higher education if they are academically qualified and if they are financially able. Indeed, as of 2014 (National Center for Education Statistics, 2016), only 34% of the U.S. population has completed an associate's or bachelor's degree by the age of 29. In addition to the choice of whether to partake of higher education, some students also have many more options regarding what to study and where to study, often spread across a much wider geographic area than any options they may have had for primary or secondary schooling.

As more students take part in high-cost higher education, particularly in the United States, there is greater emphasis on framing tertiary education as a financial investment. Many young people think, "I will spend a certain amount of money and time in exchange for the services of a particular higher education institution." When comparing costs and benefits of various options, students evaluate many aspects of the learning experience and its personal, academic, professional, and geographic fit for them. They also consider the financial costs and the benefits of the program they choose. As people make this choice, they begin to ask themselves, "If I choose to enroll in this program, what will I get out of it?"

However, is it right for us to think of higher education in this transactional way? In places such as Germany and many Scandinavian countries, public funding for higher education creates an environment in which individuals are less financially burdened by supporting their own education. Is higher education less transactional in those contexts? If so, is that a positive thing?

THE TRANSACTIONAL NATURE OF HIGHER EDUCATION

It is clear that higher education has always been based, at some level, on a financial transaction. A student—or some scholarship benefactor—pays

Figure 8.1. Two Global Trends Shifting Higher Education Transactional View of Higher Education

Level	Forces	Result
A. Institutional	Declining state appropriations, increasing costs, higher enrollment/demand.	Institutions viewing students as profit centers
B. Personal	Different needs for jobs, high rates of student loans, and unemployment.	Return-to-investment (ROI) lens

tuition in exchange for the opportunity to study through a particular institution. Even in places such as Denmark, Finland, or Slovenia where tertiary education is free or heavily subsidized, students are supported by some combination of guaranteed low-interest loans and grants. However, while this transactional view of higher education has always been present, there has been a notable shift in the stakes of higher education over the past three decades such that this transactional view has come to eclipse all else.

We see two trends (Figure 8.1) as having pushed stakeholders, that is students, families, higher education institutions, and government, to consider higher education in this way. First, the increase of costs within higher education institutions and the decline in public appropriations over the past few decades have forced institutions to act in a market-centric way, particularly in the view of students as potential profit centers. Second, the rapid rise of loan debt and increased competitiveness have encouraged students to view higher education through a return-on-investment lens.

The Institutional View of Students as Profit Centers

Contemporary higher education is undeniably a big business due to the increasing number of students attending college, as well as the greater amount of student loan burden taken on by individuals and families. Over the past two decades, the number of participants in higher education globally has risen dramatically; tertiary student participation expanded by over 50% between 2000 and 2007 alone (Altbach, Reisberg, & Rumbley, 2009). Accompanying this explosive growth is the need to build institutional capacity to support a diverse range of students. It is estimated that postsecondary institutions in the United States received a total of $497 billion in total revenue in 2009, equivalent to

3.6% of the gross domestic product (GDP), including $144 billion in federal grants and loans (Department of the Treasury and Department of Education, 2012). It is clear that ensuring sufficient revenue to support these students and their accompanying educational costs must be a central concern for universities. However, in the contemporary global economy, there is an increasing trend for student tuition revenue to be seen as a priority and not just a means to the end of educational improvement.

At one extreme are private for-profit universities, which exist specifically to generate financial returns and profits from students. The fact that such institutions exist suggests that there is a population of students whose needs aren't being met by traditional nonprofit private and public higher education institutions. Some for-profit universities do indeed ethically enable students to access programs that they otherwise couldn't, and some students do graduate successfully from these programs with the ability to pursue higher-paying jobs or further education. However, many such institutions have extremely low completion rates, high levels of debt for outgoing students, and student loan default rates that are substantially higher than other institutions. It is typically the case that incoming students are less qualified to begin with, which explains some of these discrepancies. However, when students enroll, take on debt, and fail to graduate successfully, they are often worse off financially than if they had never enrolled. Several for-profit colleges have also used illegal recruiting practices to bring in additional students (Deming, Goldin, & Katz, 2013). Here, the revenue that comes with each student is the priority, not necessarily learning outcomes.

However, such a focus on revenue is not unique to for-profit colleges. Nonprofit private and public higher education institutions are also focusing more deeply on revenue out of necessity to sustain themselves. In an era of declining state funding for higher education, a focus on the bottom line has become more urgent. According to the American Council of Education (Mortenson, 2012), with the exception of North Dakota and Wyoming, all states have reduced their support for higher education by anywhere from 14.8 to 69.4% between fiscal 1980 and fiscal 2011. In response, nonprofit higher education institutions have pursued multiple means of cost cutting. This has taken the form of increasing reliance on adjunct and graduate student faculty or cutting courses and departments (Oliff, Palacios, Johnson, & Leachman, 2013). In addition, nonprofit institutions have become more intentional about seeking revenue streams, particularly in student enrollment.

The search for stable income for American colleges and universities has also expanded internationally, at times resulting in controversy. In 2016, the *New York Times* (Saul, 2016) reported on several cases of

American universities attempting to recruit full-tuition-paying international students to their campuses by working with foreign companies with questionable marketing practices and misaligned financial incentives. In addition to concerns about false advertising, many students recruited in this way were found not to be academically or linguistically qualified to be successful in the U.S. universities to which they were subsequently admitted. Higher education institutions may have valid pedagogical reasons for recruiting international students and often do so in legitimate ways, but without doubt, revenue potential is at least part of this push, which—even in situations that aren't clearly unethical—raises questions about the extent to which students should be thought of as profit centers. When a university tries to recruit potential students likely to bring in generous amounts of tuition revenue, it is understandable that questions arise as to the university's alignment with its declared educational motivation.

This focus on international students as sources of revenue is not unique to higher education institutions. Governments are also increasingly aware of the financial implications of the enrollment of international students. This is part of a growing trend in which nations' economic perspectives are increasingly counting on higher education to not only prepare citizens to be competitive in the global workforce, but to be an exportable service to other nations.

An export/import framework generally refers to goods or services that are being produced in one country and sold to buyers from a foreign country. Australia, for example, is a major exporter of education. When international students enroll in an Australian university, that university is essentially selling education as a service to students from other countries, although the recipients of such service actually move to Australia to receive it.

The trade balance in higher education can have major economic implications for exporting and importing nations. Nearly 600,000 full-fee-paying international students were enrolled in postsecondary institutions in Australia in 2014 and collectively generated $11.7 billion Australian dollars (or $9 billion U.S.) in income for Australia (Xinhuanet News, 2015). This makes international higher education Australia's largest service export and fourth largest export of any kind, only exceeded by iron ore, coal, and natural gas. Similarly, international students contributed more than $30.5 billion to the U.S. economy in the academic year 2014–2015 (Zong & Batalova, 2016). On the other hand, China undeniably became the largest importing country, sending nearly half a million students to the United States, UK, Australia, and other countries for tertiary education as of 2014. Among those students, 92% were self-funded.

As higher education costs rise, educational institutions and national governments are increasingly viewing students as potential revenue sources and are thinking about higher education as a key national industry economically. In many ways, the large spending on higher education can be beneficial because increased spending on higher education can lead to higher access to tertiary education and better quality. There are concerns, however, about what that money is being spent on, the quality of the learning that takes place, and who specifically takes on the financial burden of education. When governments and educational institutions increasingly place this burden on students in the form of loans, this also pushes students to think of higher education in increasingly financial terms—the second key factor in the increasing preeminence of the transactional view of higher education.

The Assumption That Quality Is Reducible to Students' Financial Return on Investment (ROI)

So far, we have looked at the financial costs of higher education and how students, higher education institutions, and national economies view the economic impact of spending on student tuition and fees. From the student's perspective, increasing rates of tuition coupled with low average salaries and higher rates of unemployment for college graduates have led to an increased focus on the economic outputs of higher education in the form of students' personal earning potential (Davis, Kimball, & Gould, 2015). Indeed, the rises of loan debt and increased competitiveness have encouraged students to view higher education through a return-on-investment lens. Hunter Rawlings, former president of Cornell University and the University of Iowa, has echoed the critiques of many university leaders to this phenomenon in his recent provocative *Washington Post* article. "Most public discussion of higher education today," writes Rawlings, "pretends that students simply receive their education from colleges the way a person walks out of Best Buy with a television" (Rawlings, 2015). Rather than fostering an environment where students produce critical thought in front of a class, Rawlings and others have suggested that the students-as-customer and institution-as-provider model has changed the higher education experience for the worse.

Rawlings' statements do indeed align with the ways in which many students and families view higher education. In the United States in 2011, 86% of poll respondents (English, 2011) said the main reason students go to college is to earn more money or to get a good job. There is much truth to this. Many people certainly do dramatically increase

their earning potential with each additional degree, and unemployment or underemployment rates are substantially lower for students
with a college degree. On the other hand, it is important to note that
it is not clear if going to college is causing these differences in earning
potential and employment rates. However, at the heart of Rawlings'
and others' criticisms is that employment prospects have been touted
by many as the primary purpose of higher education. Students try
to enroll in programs they think will lead to financial success, institutions tout earnings of graduates, and governments push the mac-
roeconomic benefits of more graduates and higher-paying jobs. For
example, at the National Governors Association Meeting (The White
House, 2012) in February 2012, President Obama addressed higher
education as an area demanding our immediate focus because of the
growing need for more highly educated workers to fill the jobs of
the future. State-level rhetoric is even more pointed. Florida Governor
Rick Scott (AACRAO, 2015) sought to link public funding to job outcomes by famously saying, "If I'm going to take money from a citizen
to put into education, then I'm going to take that money to create
jobs. So, I want that money to go to degrees where people can get jobs
in the state. Is it a vital interest of the state to have more anthropolo-
gists? I don't think so."

This focus on practical employment outcomes is not unique to the
United States. For example, Namibia's National Council for Higher
Education is explicit about their goal of ensuring that graduates have
skills that are responsive and relevant to the market demand and that
the higher education institutions develop future employees who are well
versed in recent trends in the job market in order to drive growth and
development.

Taking the focus on students' future financial outcomes to its logical
extreme, several organizations, such as PayScale, rate institutions' financial return on investment (ROI) based on students who attend. Business
magazine Forbes ranks universities based on the idea that the best colleges are those that produce successful people who make enough money
during their careers to be charitable and feel compelled to give back to
their alma mater (Forbes, 2016). This makes the private, not-for-profit
college business model look like it is all about admitting and producing
the best crop of future donors. Ironically, Forbes published an opinion
piece in 2015 by Troy Onink that critiques ROI rankings done by organizations such as by Forbes itself (Onink, 2015). This article argued that
rankings based on average ROI are not particularly useful, since there
is so much individual variation, and provided some suggested ways of
evaluating a student's own personal ROI. Even this critique, however,

maintained the underlying assumption that a student's ROI is what is important.

Students aren't wrong to consider their own earnings, just like institutions aren't wrong to consider their bottom line, and nations aren't wrong to want a favorable trade balance, but when the stakes in terms of professional necessity to pursue higher education and the costs and the subsequent debt for doing so are so high, this transactional focus on higher education can supersede deeper pedagogical and developmental goals people have for higher education. Financial considerations may come to the forefront and supersede nations' wider societal goals in terms of enhancing public good and developing wise citizens.

INTERNATIONAL ALTERNATIVES

We have now examined the two trends spurring the transactional view of higher education in the United States. To what extent are these forces at play internationally? Have governments and institutions in other countries responded in similar ways? Prominent American politicians and lawmakers have also been asking these questions, many of them turning toward European systems as models. For example, 2016 Democratic presidential candidate Bernie Sanders, citing the highly competitive global economy and the mountain of debt that currently burdens American students, has argued that free, public 4-year college is not a radical idea (Sanders, 2016). Sanders states that "Germany eliminated tuition because they believed that charging students $1,300 per year was discouraging Germans from going to college. . . . Finland, Norway, Sweden, and many other countries around the world also offer free college to all of their citizens." It is worth noting that these countries each make different tradeoffs in order to provide such opportunities to students. As economics reporter Matt Phillips (2013) puts it, "Student debt is just our solution for an age-old problem. It's society's way of financing a restructuring period for the currently unproductive assets it will depend on in the future: young people". Other countries have other solutions, each with their own pros and cons.

Sweden is one of the seven countries that offers totally tuition-free higher education to its citizens. Graduating with a combined six digits of debt, we have dreamed about the glories of moving to Sweden and obtaining a degree from a high-quality research university or college free of debt. However, we realized our naiveté after learning that these students graduate with a high debt burden due to Sweden's high living expenses and a tradition of students' independence from parents' support.

In fact, 85% of Swedish students graduate with debt compared to only 50% in the United States. Moreover, new Swedish graduates have the highest debt-to-income ratios of any group in the developed world at about 80%. Simply adopting the Swedish college-free model does not automatically alleviate student debt burden.

Like Sweden, many educators and policymakers, especially those from the United States and the UK, have set Germany as an exemplar. After announcing its free university system in 2014, Germany received much public attention, mostly favorable. While questioning why other countries can't scrap tuitions fees, it is worth examining how Germany manages to do so and whether the United States could do the same. Policy analyst Mark Huelsman (ATTN Staff, 2015) argues that two key factors enable Germany to do this. "First, they simply agree to pay higher taxes. Second, Germany has a lower percentage of students go on to college than we have here in the United States." More importantly, residential college life, large stadiums, and small classrooms are not usually seen in German universities. Only comparing the German university system to the United States misses how German society structures trades, employment, professional training, and education. In Germany, higher education has a clear binary differentiation between universities and institutions of engineering, medicine, economics, and various colleges and vocational schools.

All things considered, it seems that this is a win-win situation for Germany because nearly 50% of all foreign students stay in the country after graduation, paying taxes and providing the labor market with skilled workers. More than 10,000 U.S. students are presently enrolled in Germany's higher education programs, according to data from the Institute for International Education. This is an increase of almost 9% compared to the previous academic year and 25% more than in 2008–2009 (Institute of International Education, 2015).

CONCLUSION

Students, families, institutions, states, and nations all feel pressure to think of higher education in increasingly transactional ways by viewing students as revenue centers and assuming quality is reducible to students' financial return on investment. The risk is that these forces diminish the essential, transformative nature of higher education. While judging universities on the average salaries of their graduates might be a better way to assess quality than, say, how big and fancy a school's athletic center is, it still misses out on many other factors, which may not be well-captured in financial terms, that make higher education an important human experience. It ignores the inherent value of getting to meet and learn with people from different backgrounds, getting to experience new cities and countries, developing lifelong personal and professional friendships, and exploring new areas of interest. It also ignores the community benefits of a more informed citizenry and the public benefits of graduates taking on lower-paying but critically important careers in the education or nonprofit sectors, for example.

Examining other higher education systems, such as Sweden and Germany, has shown that there are often significant societal assumptions, values, and even tradeoffs in creating a free tertiary education system. U.S. colleges and universities would need to enroll fewer 4-year students and instead create a high-quality system of vocational and technical education that would offer competitive alternatives to those students whose aspirations are more about learning knowledge and skills that qualify for specific jobs. Many European countries have done exactly this to make higher education accessible and affordable to those who desire to choose such a pathway.

Reflecting on our own situation as soon-to-be graduates carrying substantial debt, we acknowledge the necessity of viewing higher education as a transaction. It is a huge industry, and our own education will more than likely have a major impact on our future earnings. However, this doesn't necessarily have to be an obstacle to higher education achieving its ideals, since it can, in fact, design transformative learning experiences for students within its wider transactional context. For example, Denison University, a small liberal arts college in Ohio, has recently created a new global commerce major. Denison is focused on inspiring and educating its students to become autonomous thinkers, discerning moral agents, and active citizens of a democratic society. However, in designing the new global commerce major, it has acknowledged the transactional pre-professional importance of undergraduate education, and it has sought to use students' professional interests to enhance their liberal arts learning and use liberal arts learning to enhance their professional pursuits. For example, while studying global commerce, a transactional topic itself, students learn languages, engage with students and scholars across the world, study economic systems, and critique power structures—all very deep aspects of the liberal arts. Denison has thus rejected the false choice between a transactional view of higher education (in this case, improving students' future job prospects and financial ROI) and its core educational values.

As the financial stakes grow, it becomes increasingly challenging to maintain this focus on the real learning. Rather than bemoan the transactional nature of higher education, we can focus instead on ensuring that this doesn't overwhelm the deeper purposes of higher education. We must simultaneously focus on accessibility, quality, and affordability of higher education in order to ensure that higher education can continue to prioritize its focus on the development of people, not just current customers and future workers.

REFERENCES

AACRAO. (2015). Republican governors' shared goals for higher ed: accountability and work-force preparation. Retrieved from http://www.aacrao.org/resources/resources-detail-view/republican-governors--shared-goals-for-higher-ed-accountability-and-work-force-preparation

Altbach, P. G., Reisberg, L., & Rumbley, L. E. (2009). *Trends in global higher education: Tracking an academic revolution.* Paris: UNESCO. Retrieved from http://s3.amazonaws.com/academia.edu.documents/30910755/Altbach__Reisberg__Rumbley_Tracking_an_Academic_Revolution__UNESCO_2009.pdf?AWSAccessKeyId=AKIAJ56TQJRTWSMTNPEA&Expires=1474212382&Signature=TYbQ%2BSeT5ojIURs4Y9dSSs9w%2FaY%3D&response-content-disposition=inline%3B%20filename%3DTrends_in_global_higher_education_Tracki.pdf

ATTN Staff. (2015). How does Germany afford free tuition for all of its citizens? (March 27). Retrieved from http://www.attn.com/stories/211/how-does-germany-afford-free-tuition-all-its-citizens

Cronon, W. (1998). Only connect. . . . The goals of a liberal education. *American Scholar, 67*(4).

Davis, A., Kimball, W., & Gould, E. (2015). *The class of 2015: Despite an improving economy, young grads still face an uphill climb.* Retrieved from http://www.epi.org/publication/the-class-of-2015/

Deming, D., Goldin, C., & Katz, L. (2013). For-profit colleges. *The Future of Children, 23*(1). Retrieved from http://scholar.harvard.edu/files/goldin/files/for-profit_colleges.pdf

Department of the Treasury and Department of Education. (2012). *The economics of higher education.* Washington, DC: Department of Treasury. Retrieved from https://www.treasury.gov/connect/blog/Documents/20121212_Economics of Higher Ed_vFINAL.pdf Retrieved from https://www.treasury.gov/connect/blog/Documents/20121212_Economics of Higher Ed_vFINAL.pdf

English, C. (2011). *Most Americans see college as essential to getting a good job.* Retrieved from http://www.gallup.com/poll/149045/americans-college-essential-getting-good-job.aspx

Forbes. (2016, July). *The colleges ranking: the full methodology.* Retrieved from http://www.forbes.com/sites/carolinehoward/2016/07/06/top-colleges-ranking-2016-the-full-methodology/#550e83a459a8

Howard, M. (2013). Foreword. In M. Fennell, & S. Miller (Eds.), *Responding to the commoditization of higher education.* Retrieved from http://www.presidentialperspectives.org/pdf/2013/2013-chapter-0-and-1-against-the-windmills-he-commoditization-cevallos.pdf

Institute of International Education. (2015). Top 25 Destinations of U.S. Study Abroad Students, 2012/13--2013/14. *Open Doors Report on International Educational Exchange.* Retrieved from http://www.iie.org/opendoors

Mortenson, T. G. (2012). *State funding: A race to the bottom.* Retrieved from http://www.acenet.edu/the-presidency/columns-and-features/Pages/state-funding-a-race-to-the-bottom.aspx

Oliff, P., Palacios, V., Johnson, I., & Leachman, M. (2013). *Recent deep state higher education cuts may harm students and the economy for years to come.* Retrieved from http://www.cbpp.org/sites/default/files/atoms/files/3-19-13sfp.pdf

Onink, T. (2015). *Unless you're average, college ROI and best value rankings are misleading.* Retrieved from http://www.forbes.com/sites/troyonink/2015/07/31/unless-your-average-college-roi-and-best-value-rankings-are-a-waste-of-time/#6c76bea5684f

Phillips, M. (2013, May). The high price of a free college education in Sweden. *The Atlantic.* Retrieved from http://www.theatlantic.com/international/archive/2013/05/the-high-price-of-a-free-college-education-in-sweden/276428/?utm_source=atlfb

Rawlings, H. (2015). *College is not a commodity stop treating it like one.* Retrieved from https://www.washingtonpost.com/posteverything/wp/2015/06/09/college-is-not-a-commodity-stop-treating-it-like-one/

The White House. (2012). Remarks by the president at national governors' association meeting. Retrieved from https://www.whitehouse.gov/the-press-office/2012/02/27/remarks-president-national-governors-association-meeting

Sanders, B. (2016). *It is time to make college tuition free and debt free.* Retrieved from https://berniesanders.com/issues/its-time-to-make-college-tuition-free-and-debt--free/

Saul, S. (2016). *Recruiting students overseas to fill seats, not to meet standards.* Retrieved from http://www.nytimes.com/2016/04/20/us/recruiting-students-overseas-to-fill-seats-not-to-meet-standards.html?_r=0

National Center for Education Statistics. (2016). The condition of education 2016 (2016, May). Retrieved from http://nces.ed.gov/pubs2016/2016144.pdf

Xinhuanet News. (2015). International education earns Australia 17.6 bln AU dollars in 2014. Retrieved from http://news.xinhuanet.com/english/2015-06/22/c_134346610.htm

Zong, J., & Batalova, J. (2016). *International students in the United States.* Retrieved from http://www.migrationpolicy.org/article/international-students-united-states

CHAPTER 9

What Can We Learn from Hard Questions?

The authors of the preceding chapters have tried to articulate why hard questions are needed in the global education reform debate and why generating new questions from them—not just answers—is sometimes more helpful than being right or winning the debate. Therefore, this concluding chapter will not close with the final answers and synthesis of the preceding chapters. Instead, we outline emerging thoughts after working for full academic year with our students, reading what they wrote, and thinking about how it resonates with our own thinking about educational change in the United States and beyond. Focus in the following paragraphs is deliberately placed on education policies and practices in the United States, with the understanding that similar conclusions could have been made about many other countries around the work and their education systems.

THE IMPORTANCE OF COHERENCE

It is nearly impossible to reach a consensus in the United States on the purpose of public education. No social contract exists between our government and its students. National education agendas are not entirely contingent on previous policies, and departments of education, states, and local school boards all behave differently. Perhaps it is only possible to say that too many reforms have led to confusion and frustration among stakeholders instead of a shared understanding of how and how not to improve schools.

Marc Tucker of the National Center on Education and the Economy (NCEE) attributes this confusion and frustration to reformers constantly adding programs to the corpus of programs already in place (Tucker, 2011). As a result of this pattern, U.S. schools often spend inordinate amounts of time figuring out how to implement these numerous reforms instead of spending energy and resources on actually strengthening and improving teaching and learning. Similar overdose of education reform initiatives has occurred throughout other OECD countries as well. OECD's Beatriz Pont mentioned in her lecture at the Graduate School of Education in October 2015 that more than 450 reforms were rolled out between 2008 and 2014.

This appears especially true at a national level in the United States. Initially, there was the No Child Left Behind Act (NCLB), passed during the George W. Bush administration, which pushed a level of account-ability into schooling meant to, in the president's words, "combat the soft bigotry of low expectations" (*Washington Post*, 2004). The law stipulated that by 2014 all students had to be proficient in grade-level math and reading, which meant that schools had to implement instruc-tional strategies, new curricula, and professional development sessions towards meeting this lofty goal.

Not surprisingly, NCLB reform soon became a euphemism for assigning blame: on teachers who couldn't get their students to meet state benchmarks, on schools that were substituting instruction for test preparation, and on politicians whose well-intentioned legislation was not, in fact, leading to improved teaching or learning. Accountability, the main pillar of NCLB meant to increase student performance, had instead become a license for finger pointing.

President Obama's solution for dealing with states that were not on pace to meet the 100% proficiency benchmark was issuing waivers to 45 states (Center on Education Policy, n.d.), which exempted them from central provisions. In exchange for relief, states had to promise they would create new targets focused on college and career readiness for all students, one of the main tenets of President Obama's signature education program, Race to the Top (RTTT). While these waivers pro-tected states from being labeled failures and the severe sanctions that came with that designation, it also changed incentives for school lead-ers. Overwhelmed principals and teachers now had to make sure they were pushing students towards grade-level proficiency, preparing them for college and career, and ensuring that test scores would prove their efficacy as educators.

Consider the perverse consequences that befell the state of Ver-mont (Holcombe, 2014). Even though the National Assessment of

Education Progress (NAEP) consistently ranked Vermont one of the higher performing states in the nation, and the Trends in International Mathematics and Science Study ranked Vermont seventh in the world in 8th-grade mathematics, the U.S. Department of Education labeled nearly every school in Vermont as failing. Vermont's Secretary of Education Rebecca Holcombe made headlines for refusing a waiver from the Obama administration, in part because her administration did not trust replacing one bad accountability provision (every student must be labeled proficient) with what they deemed to be another (teachers would be evaluated using student test scores).

Cases such as Vermont reveal how easy it is for well-intentioned reforms to send mixed messages to communities and why the Every Student Succeeds Act (ESSA), which replaced NCLB in 2016, still does nothing to clarify the hard question that legislation is trying to answer. This type of incoherence has serious consequences for schools, and perhaps it results from a lack of a clear question.

THE IMPORTANCE OF COLLABORATION

For all the hand wringing around incoherence, the absence of infrastructure to support teacher and student collaboration might be the most concerning. The unintended cost from district, state, and federal accountability provisions has forced educators to sacrifice collaborative opportunities so that they can prioritize teaching to the test. Even value-added measures, which were encouraged under RTTT, focus on an individual teacher's impact on the growth of her students, not the host of other teachers by which a student might be influenced over the course of their academic career.

The pressure from top-down accountability has removed much of the incentives for teachers to share responsibility to improve anything besides their own students' growth. This is perhaps the biggest difference between U.S. public schools and high-performing international systems in countries such as Finland, Canada, Estonia, and Singapore. These systems have made deliberate efforts and investments to carve out time for teacher collaboration.

Unfortunately, U.S. policies have almost exclusively abandoned collaboration, and in so doing, they have adversely impacted schools. High teacher attrition, for example, is in part related to a perception of a teaching profession that is isolating, where teachers are left alone in their classrooms to fend for themselves. Because of these working conditions, the National Education Association reports that half of new teachers in the United States leave the profession within 5 years, while the annual MetLife Survey of the American Teacher (2013) reveals teacher morale in the United States at its lowest since 1991.

Opportunities for teachers to engage in deep collaboration are rare in a political environment that is quick to assign blame for failing schools and even quicker to use accountability measures to undermine many of the roles teachers are forced to undertake. The 2015 criminal case accusing 12 former Atlanta Public School (Blinder, 2015) employees and the former superintendent of cheating was a sad reminder that current accountability provisions in federal and now state statutes that do not incentivize collaboration have not worked as designed and have failed teachers and students. Without incentives for teacher collaboration, the perception of the profession will continue to suffer, and teachers will continue to be expected to overcome student challenges on their own.

Student collaboration is also a critical consideration in forming hard questions for education reform. Failure is always a possible by-product of collaboration. However, this is not a desired option for U.S. schools. Students should be encouraged to take risks and work together on projects to demonstrate their skills. Perseverance, grit, and problem-solving skills are all qualities that often come from struggling to overcome past failures. Not surprisingly, these are the same skills employers cite as attractive in their new hires.

Looking abroad, respecting the need for teachers to collaborate has provided Finnish teachers not only the space to improve their content knowledge and pedagogy but also a support system where their professional improvement is connected to their school improvement.

THE IMPORTANCE OF MULTIPLE POSTSECONDARY PATHWAYS

Young people with more education earn more than those with less education, yet the $1.2 trillion in student loan debt and the elimination of millions of high-skilled jobs over the last decade casts considerable doubt that educational attainment is still a guarantee for gainful employment. All this makes it difficult to reconcile college and career readiness as a vision for students if college is not affordable for every student and if student loans are too onerous for young adults.

Given the misalignment between academic and employability skills, it is particularly concerning when reformers advocate a college-for-all mantra. This message, popular in charter movements such as Knowledge is Power Program (KIPP) schools and programs such as Teach for America, inadvertently blocks alternative postsecondary pathways for many students who do not aspire to attend 4-year programs. Whether young people don't believe 4-year colleges offer them the most cost-effective investment in today's economy, or they simply prefer work over school, U.S. schools have not paved pathways for students with different college and career goals. As a result, students can make short-term decisions without understanding the full scope of long-term opportunities they may forgo, such as dropping out of school or not pursuing postsecondary schooling at all.

The troubling part about the college-for-all movement is that it is myopic to the fact that many young people would benefit tremendously from alternative pathways for academic continuation and workforce preparedness. However, these alternative programs—specifically vocational schools and career and technical education programs—suffer from a pejorative perception and reality in the United States as places where low-income children and children of color are consigned to a second-rate education.

Once again, education systems such as Switzerland, Finland, and Singapore demonstrate the benefits from investing in multiple post secondary tracks. Both countries worked hard to transform the image of vocational education through investments in technical campuses equipped with high-tech facilities, new curricula, and workforce certification systems. In transferring from labor-intensive and export-oriented economies to skill-based economies, the Finnish and Singaporean governments approached reform by deciding to offer multiple pathways to students. These pathways became so popular in Finland that 43% of high school students attend vocational school (Jackson & Hasak, 2014). Similarly, in Singapore, after acquiring a strong academic foundation in their early schooling experience, students are allowed to pursue one of three types of high schools: a traditional academic track that prepares students for postsecondary education, a polytechnic track that focuses on advanced occupational and technical training, and a technical institute that focuses on less-advanced occupational and technical training.

What is compelling about both models is that they were not created as placeholders for non-college-bound youth but instead were offered as popular alternatives for postsecondary education.

Even President Obama's community college proposal in early 2015 signaled an important step at a public makeover for alternative pathways that could help younger Americans gain postsecondary experience and skills leading to gainful employment. Considering that the share of young people enrolling in any college has begun to decline, this has been a welcome change of course (Casselman, 2014). Still, much more political let alone financial investments are needed.

It is difficult to imagine parents asking their schools to help support sending their student to a campus with outdated facilities or to a program where teachers are not equipped to provide academic and technical support, yet, as skills have become the global currency of 21st century economies, it is clear that having one postsecondary pathway has produced inequitable opportunities for students. Without multiple postsecondary pathways and explicit connections made between coursework and careers, students are likely to remain disengaged and discouraged by a message that says college is their best chance for a life of success.

The chapters in this book have reframed problems in the global education reform movement not simply to offer simple answers to the reader. In order for us all to strengthen schools across the world and improve labor markets and life outcomes for our students, we might have to resist the urge to offer another answer and instead work first to understand the question we want to answer.

THE IMPORTANCE OF THE FUTURE

Understanding and having deeper conversations about hard question on educational change helps to solve current problems that prevent many education systems from moving the needle. Successful education systems differ from those that are struggling to get better in the ways that these essential questions are dealt with in the home countries' politics and in public debates. Higher-performing education systems invest in understanding the purpose of education and then set a shared, inspiring vision for the future of schooling. Good examples of these education systems are the Canadian province of Alberta, Singapore, and Finland.

However, education is a dynamic process, forever changing as the world and its societies evolve. Even the most successful educational systems face unanticipated hard questions as new challenges arise. It is not only important for educators to contend with the hard questions that arise from studying the current available data, but in addition, change-makers must anticipate questions that will arise in the future.

For example, the increasingly global nature of the world and its conflicts have begun to disrupt historically homogenous educational systems. This can be seen in Finland where refugee children from Syria present new challenges to their highly successful but homogenous educational systems. As global conflicts continue to drive the growth of minority populations in more countries, issues of race and equity, long grappled with in the United States, will become far more global challenges. Moreover, the increasing diversity of what we mean by race and equity promises to push the conversation well beyond the traditional black versus white categorizations. Large migrations of Latinos, new recognition for the lesbian, gay, bisexual, and transgender (LGBT) community, and other less traditionally considered minorities will only accelerate the importance of how educational systems handle these new stakeholders.

Similarly, as countries such as United Kingdom, Australia and the United States surpass a decade of reform based on accountability, standards, and the global fixation on data-driven evaluation, there are growing concerns about its impact on the mental health of kids, parents, and educators. The pressure, anxiety, and scrutiny of educational performance—long a hallmark of educational systems across Asia and hypothesized as a contributor to their relatively high suicide rates and depression—are increasingly a global phenomenon. Relevant to many of the global trends outlined in this book, New York City recently launched the ThriveNYC initiative in an effort to raise attention and improve the mental health of the nation's largest city (Understanding New York City's mental health challenge, n.d.). A key component of the ThriveNYC program is a partnership with the NYC Department of Education to provide parents and teachers from diverse backgrounds with mental health coping skills as a way to teach their kids skills for succeeding in the modern data-driven, high-stakes educational environment.

As education continues to grapple with current and burgeoning hard questions, programs such as ThriveNYC will be needed to help all educational stakeholders—students, parents, teachers, administrators, and policymakers—adapt to global trends. Moreover, continued vigilance is required to avoid losing sight of the new questions that will inevitably arise as our economies, politics, demographics, and environment continue to shift.

We hope the chapters and the questions discussed in this book help build capacity in future changemakers to reimagine an education system that is untethered to political constraints. Too often, we think, politicians and authorities deal with hard questions on educational change without considering how different scenarios about futures of school would influence these questions.

REFERENCES

Blinder, A. (2015, April 1). *Atlanta educators convicted in school cheating scandal.* [Press release]. Retrieved from http://www.nytimes.com/2015/04/02/us/verdict-reached-in-atlanta-school-testing-trial.html?_r=0

Casselman, B. (2014, April 22). *More high school grads decide college isn't worth it.* [Blog post]. Retrieved from http://fivethirtyeight.com/features/more-high-school-grads-decide-college-isnt-worth-it/

Center on Education Policy. (n.d.). *Home page.* Retrieved from http://www.cep-dc.org/index.cfm?DocumentSubTopicID=48#Tracking

Holcombe, R. (2014). *Vermont's commitment to continuous improvement.* Retrieved from http://education.vermont.gov/sites/aoe/files/documents/edu-data-ayp-memo-parents-2014.pdf

Jackson, J. H., & Hasak, J. (2014, Fall). *Reframing, reimagining, and reinvesting in CTE.* [Blog post]. Retrieved from http://www.aft.org/ae/fall2014/jackson_hasak

MetLife Survey of the American Teacher (2013, February) Retrieved from https://www.metlife.com/assets/cao/foundation/MetLife-Teacher-Survey-2012.pdf

National Education Association (2015). Research spotlight on recruiting and retaining highly qualified teachers. Retrieved from http://www.nea.org/tools/17054.htm

Tucker, M. (2011). Researching other countries' education systems. *Surpassing Shanghai: An agenda for American education built on the world's leading systems.* Cambridge, MA: Harvard Education Press.

Understanding New York City's mental health challenge. (n.d.) Retrieved from http://www1.nyc.gov/nyc-resources/thrivenyc.page

Washington Post. (2004, May 2). President Bush's acceptance speech to the Republican National Convention [Press release]. Retrieved from http://www.washingtonpost.com/wp-dyn/articles/A57466-2004Sep2.html

INDEX

About the Authors

Jonathan Hasak is a manager of public policy and government affairs at Year Up. He is working to influence federal and local education and workforce development policies that can close the opportunity divide in the United States. Jonathan began his career as a behavior interventionist in the Los Angeles Unified School District. He taught English in Tel Aviv before joining Teach for America in the Bay Area. During his 3 years in the Oakland Unified School District, Jonathan worked as a special education teacher, a coordinator of intervention, and a teacher on special assignment. Jonathan also worked for the Office of Data and Accountability in the Boston Public Schools, where he provided professional development and data analysis to school leaders. He earned his MA in education policy and management at Harvard's Graduate School of Education and his BA from Bard College in literature and creative writing. Jonathan has published more than a dozen articles and op-eds and frequently writes about the job skills gap, the need for more cross-sector collaboration in education, and the importance of career readiness in education reform.

Vanessa Rodriguez, Ed.D. is an assistant professor in the Center for Early Childhood Health and Development in the Department of Population Health at the NYU School of Medicine. She received her doctorate in human development and education at Harvard University. Vanessa earned a master's degree in education policy and management from Harvard and a master's of science in education from the City College of New York. She also spent over a decade teaching in NYC public schools. Her current research and teaching is grounded in Mind, Brain, and Education, focusing on the social-emotional cognition and development of teachers. Vanessa is the author of the popular education book *The Teaching Brain*, and is invited to speak on this topic around the world. For more information about her work or to contact her, please visit www.teachingbrain.com.

Pasi Sahlberg, PhD, is a writer, researcher, speaker, and a visiting professor at Arizona State University. He is the author of the Grawemeyer Award–winning *Finnish Lessons,* now in its second edition. Dr. Sahlberg is the former director general of CIMO (Centre for International Mobility) at the Finnish Ministry of Education and Culture as well as a former visiting professor at Harvard University's Graduate School of Education. He has worked as a schoolteacher, a teacher educator, and an educational policy advisory in Finland and as an education expert for several international organizations and consulting firms, including the World Bank, Organisation for Economic Co-operation and Development (OECD), the European Commission, and UN organizations. During the last 2 decades, he has analyzed education reforms around the world and worked with education leaders in the United States, Canada, Europe, Australia, the Middle East, Africa, and Asia. Dr. Sahlberg was a former staff member of the World Bank in Washington, DC, and the European Training Foundation in Turin, Italy. In addition to winning the 2013 Grawemeyer in the United States, he won the 2012 Education Award in Finland, the 2014 Robert Owen Award in Scotland, and the 2016 Lego Prize. For more information and updates on this book, please visit www.pasisahlberg.com and follow in Twitter @pasi_sahlberg.